FILM THEORY

THE BASICS

D0144829

"Many introductions to film theory confuse and confound the beginner. Kevin McDonald's addition to Routledge's 'The Basics' is different. It is one of the most accessible introductions to film theory currently available, and should become the first stop for students embarking on any future study of film theory."

Warren Buckland, Oxford Brookes University, UK

Film Theory: The Basics provides an accessible introduction to the key theorists, concepts, and debates that have shaped the study of moving images. It examines film theory from its emergence in the early twentieth century to its study in the present day, and explores why film has drawn special attention as a medium, as a form of representation, and as a focal point in the rise of modern visual culture.

The book emphasizes how film theory has developed as a historically contingent discourse, one that has evolved and changed in conjunction with different social, political, and intellectual factors. To explore this fully, the book is broken down into the following distinct sections:

- Theory before theory, 1915–60
- French theory, 1949–68
- Screen theory, 1969–96
- Post-theory, 1996–2015

Complete with questions for discussion and a glossary of both key terms and key theorists, *Film Theory: The Basics* is an invaluable resource for those new to film studies and for anyone else interested in the history and significance of critical thinking in relation to the moving image.

Kevin McDonald is a lecturer in the Department of Communication Studies at California State University, Northridge where he teaches popular culture and cultural theory. His research focuses on film theory and contemporary Hollywood. He is currently co-editing a collection titled *The Netflix Effect*.

THE BASICS

FILM THEORY

THE BASICS

Kevin McDonald

Routledge
Taylor & Francis Group

LONDON AND NEW YORK

First published 2016
by Routledge
2 Park Square, Milton Park, Abingdon, Oxon OX14 4RN

and by Routledge
711 Third Avenue, New York, NY 10017

Routledge is an imprint of the Taylor & Francis Group, an informa business

British Library Cataloguing-in-Publication Data
A catalogue record for this book is available from the British Library

Library of Congress Cataloging-in-Publication Data
McDonald, Kevin, 1976–
Film theory : the basics / Kevin McDonald.
pages cm. — (The basics)
Includes bibliographical references and index.
1. Motion pictures—Philosophy. I. Title.
PN1995.M3775 2016
791.4301—dc23
2015035053

ISBN: 978-1-138-79733-8 (hbk)
ISBN: 978-1-138-79734-5 (pbk)
ISBN: 978-1-315-75719-3 (ebk)

Typeset in Bembo
by Swales & Willis Ltd, Exeter, Devon, UK

CONTENTS

ACKNOWLEDGMENTS

I would like to thank Edward Branigan and Warren Buckland for providing me with an initial opportunity to think about the history of film theory. I am very thankful to Siobhan Poole for getting this project underway. Thank you to everyone else at Routledge, especially Natalie Foster and Sheni Kruger, for seeing this book all the way to the end. I want to also thank Andrew Ritchey and Ofer Eliaz for keeping theory interesting. My biggest thank you goes to Ben Stork and Kris Fallon. This book would not have been possible without them. Finally, I want to thank my mom, Joanne, my sisters Patricia and Krista, and Gina Giotta for being there for me both before the writing begins and whenever it ends.

INTRODUCTION

For more than a century, film has drawn the interest of intellectuals, critics, artists, and scholars. Collectively, this group has asked questions about film's fundamental qualities, its distinctive features, and its various effects. These questions eventually merged with broader debates about aesthetics, technology, culture, and society. And as these exchanges became the basis for an increasingly academic form of inquiry, they fostered their own specific set of terms, methods, and rhetorical positions. Together, these developments comprise film theory; the body of writing devoted to the critical understanding of film as a medium and as a vital part of visual culture more broadly.

As a critical enterprise, film theory is relatively young. Its formation has nevertheless been wide-ranging and, at times, tumultuous. In the first part of the twentieth century, film theory consisted of a distinctly international assortment of writers and thinkers. They mostly worked in isolation from one another and approached the new medium of film from a variety of different backgrounds. They were often driven to theorize film as a matter of circumstance or out of personal interest. Sergei Eisenstein, for example, proffered theoretical views about montage as a way to both supplement and expound his own filmmaking practices. While the work of these early pioneers helped to establish the merits of moving images by the mid-point of the twentieth century, this same period saw the beginning of a fundamental shift in the direction of theoretical inquiry. The rise of structuralism, and later post-structuralism, in France laid the groundwork for new and expanded interest in semiotics, psychoanalysis, and Marxism. Although these critical discourses did not directly concern film, they came to exert tremendous influence at the same time that film study first gained traction within the Anglo-American academy during the 1970s and 1980s. Film theory has since become an important sub-field in film and media studies, but it also remains a contentious subject with many detractors questioning its intellectual worth.

Insofar as film theory has become a primarily academic endeavor, it is often considered inordinately difficult, a foreign language of sorts full of impractical and esoteric abstractions. It is certainly the case that film theory is a specialized discourse with its own distinct jargon and idiosyncratic practices. Although these features sometimes function as a deterrent, this is not necessarily by design. Film theory's complexity is due instead to several different factors. First, theory develops as part of a broader history of ideas and many of the specific terms and debates within a particular discourse bear the intricate traces of both the conceptual and institutional contexts that shaped that process. Second, theory aims to understand what is not immediately self-evident. This requires formulating a critical framework capable of discerning what otherwise exceeds or escapes existing knowledge. Third, in terms of formulating these tools, film theory has been especially conspicuous in combining elements from different practices and disciplinary rubrics.

Complicating matters further is the fact that film theory has long been divided between a descriptive or diagnostic practice devoted to evaluation and interpretation—similar to the scholarly writing done in the name of literary criticism or art history—and a more prescriptive or interventionist approach whereby theory provides the parameters necessary to found new forms of cinematic practice. In all of these different ways, however, theory deviates far from what many general readers may think of as theory in its most ordinary sense. In other words, film theory does not typically aim to provide universal principles or a comprehensive system of logically reasoned propositions that explain film or every aspect of its various implications. And for the most part even the most intricate and systematic examples of film theory cannot be reduced to standardized methods or hypotheses that are subject to empirical assessment. It is not that film theory is completely indifferent to these principles, but it is primarily a historically contingent discourse, one that is tied to a liberal humanist intellectual tradition rather than the applied sciences. As such, it comprises the ideas and arguments that have changed over time as film and its associated meanings have changed.

This may also account for the main reason that film theory remains so challenging. Both as a medium and as a practice, film is an incredibly complex and multi-faceted object of study. As a material object, film combines a transparent, synthetic plastic base coated with a light-sensitive chemical substance that, once exposed, serves as a representational record or artifact. As a late nineteenth-century invention, this new medium was a direct extension of photography, but also a byproduct of different endeavors including scientific research, developments in popular entertainment, new industrial production processes, and entrepreneurial finesse. As a practice, film predominantly refers to the moment of capture or recording of what appears before the camera. But this activity can also expand to encompass other aspects of the filmmaking process like optical printing or editing. As these practices developed into a successful commercial enterprise, film also became part of a complex industrial process. In the United States, it became the basis of a vertically integrated studio system whereby Hollywood controlled the production, distribution, and exhibition of most films. This system, alternatively known as classical Hollywood cinema, simultaneously facilitated a unique set of visual and narrative conventions, privileging things like continuity.

By the end of the twentieth century, the meaning of film had become more complicated. In some ways, film has become more diffuse, merging with competing technologies like television, video games, and the internet. The proliferation of these technologies has certainly changed the ways in which films are circulated and consumed. Though traditional theatrical exhibition still plays an important role, films today are predominantly viewed in other contexts, either on home video formats like DVD and Blu-ray or on video-on-demand platforms and internet streaming services that are accessed through personal computing devices (e.g. laptops and tablets) or mobile phones. These changes have raised serious questions for film theory. The most prominent concern is that new digital technologies have fundamentally supplanted film as a medium—replacing its physical dimensions with immaterial binary codes. On one hand, film theory has adapted to these changes by simply expanding its purview to include a wider range of visual culture, one that encompasses, for example, media, screen arts, and communication technologies in a much broader sense. On the other hand, film continues to have currency despite its apparent demise. For instance, it is still possible to hear things like, "I watched that film on TV" or "I filmed that with my phone." This means that even though film and film theory may evoke anachronism, they continue to inform our understanding of moving images and still have much to contribute in the digital age.

Film's complexity is not just the result of its changing material or discursive status, but part of its overall standing as a cultural object. Film has always been intertwined with the paradoxical implications of modern life or what is sometimes more generally termed modernity. When first invented, for instance, film was celebrated for its ability to capture and recreate movement. It was an exhilarating novelty embodying the energy and dynamism of modern technology. However, at the same time it was capable of evoking the disorientation and alienation that were equally prominent amidst rapid industrialization, urbanization, and new forms of socialization. In this respect, according to Maxim Gorky's famous early account, film depicted a gray and dismal world deprived of all vitality. These conflicting associations set the tone for a medium that has regularly brought together opposing traits. For example, film is prized for its verisimilitude and its ability to document physical reality. It is taken to be a factual, trustworthy source of evidence, and a paragon of realist representation. On the other hand, film is characterized as an optical illusion and a celebrated source of entertainment best known for its fictional scenarios. In this regard, film is more closely associated with its ability to elicit pleasure and its affinity with fantasy and distortion. These different attributes have all prompted elaborate debates about film's social and psychological effects. As part of these debates, theorists have been particularly critical of film's power to reinforce cultural beliefs and ideologies. At the same time, many theorists have extolled film as an exemplary form of modern art. In this regard they have enthusiastically embraced film's creative and political powers—though this is often the case only insofar as they are deemed capable of challenging the existing status quo.

In the long run, film's complexity and contradictory implications would have its benefits. In a sense, they are responsible for the diverse range of issues taken up by film theorists that have required increasingly sophisticated forms of analysis and debate. In the short term, however, these challenges have also created periods of disorder and disagreement. This was most clearly the case in the first half of the twentieth century as film theory began to take its initial shape. During this time, film theory consisted of a loose-knit, eclectic mix of unorthodox thinkers. Although this group was devoted to establishing film's merit, its distinctive aesthetic features, and its overall cultural legitimacy, there was very little overarching support or conceptual focus linking these early efforts together. Thus Chapter 1, "Theory before theory," details several different localized movements in the US and Europe, each of which featured its own distinct mix of film enthusiasts, filmmakers, and iconoclastic intellectuals. This was a period of innovation and exploration, fueled by pragmatic zeal and a growing appreciation for the new medium. As indispensable as this period was in laying the foundation for later work, it was also a time in which theory remained fragmentary and inchoate. It was only later, as subsequent critics and scholars began moving in new and different directions, that these early pioneers became part of what was retroactively designated classical film theory.

For many years, the simple distinction between classical film theory and contemporary film theory was considered sufficient. The former referred to an earlier generation of theorists, most of whom are covered in Chapter 1, and a period that had concluded around 1960. The latter referred to the tropes and methods that took precedence from that point on. Although this periodization is still used as a matter of convenience, it now raises as many questions as it answers. In an effort to address these concerns, this book takes a somewhat different approach to the later stages of film theory's development. While there is a strong emphasis on maintaining a chronological narrative throughout, Chapter 2 is devoted to French theory and the years between 1949 and 1968, meaning there is some overlap with the period considered in the previous chapter. This approach allows

André Bazin and Siegfried Kracauer to be included with the earlier group of theorists even as they continued to write about cinema throughout this later period. It then draws separate attention to the contemporaneous emergence of structuralism, an integral precursor and catalyst for the contemporary variation of film theory that really only gained full momentum in the 1970s.

In addition to its overview of structuralism, Chapter 2 details some of the more specific developments associated with semiotics, psychoanalysis, and Marxism that took place during this period. Although this requires something of a detour away from film in a strict sense, it is warranted considering the influence of Roland Barthes, Jacques Lacan, and Louis Althusser on later film theorists. In many regards, this group of French theorists established not only the terms and concepts that permeated film study for the next two decades, but its entire mindset. In this regard, these theorists also provided an important intellectual model, a new example of professionalized scholarship that combined methodological rigor with inter-disciplinary sophistication and anti-establishment verve.

The last two chapters cover the period more typically referred to as contemporary film theory. Chapter 3, "Screen theory," focuses on the 1970s and 1980s, the period in which film study was incorporated into the Anglophone academy. It was at this time that film theory became a formally recognized and influential intellectual discourse. A large part of this success was tied to its connection with innovations undertaken by feminist, post-colonial, and queer theorists as well as affiliated developments in cultural studies and the critical analysis of race, class, gender, and sexuality across popular culture. Chapter 4, in turn, addresses how theory has changed in the period between 1996 and 2015 amidst a growing body of criticism directed at film theory and shifting interests within the academy. During this time, and partly as a result of its entrenchment as an academic discipline, film theory has shifted much of its focus, revisiting previous periods and questioning the problems or limitations that are now apparent in theory's earlier strategies. Although this chapter takes the title of "Post-theory," it does not argue that theory has ceased to exist. In the same way that film theory came into existence prior to it being named as such, it continues to evolve even as it has lost much of its rhetorical force as a self-sufficient organizing principle. To put it another way, while film and media scholars may be less likely to invoke film theory as such, most of their research remains deeply informed by it and the most rigorous and sophisticated examples of scholarship in the field today necessarily maintain an ongoing dialogue with it and its legacy.

Film theory and this book are most likely to be encountered within a university setting as a required class or field of knowledge that must be learned as a matter of one's course of study. This book is an introductory text that aims to be of assistance in this context. Its primary objective is to make the complex history and diverse implications of film theory accessible to students, as well as general readers. It presents a predominantly chronological account of film theory and, true to the academic nature of the topic, highlights the key terms, debates, and figures that have shaped the field. Each chapter surveys a distinct historical period of development that coheres around certain common conceptual and practical concerns. In addition to the shared attitudes and priorities that are evident across the work of individual theorists, each stage bears traces of its surrounding social-historical circumstances. To this end, there is some effort to situate the development of film theory within a broader historical and intellectual context, and as part of contemporaneous debates about aesthetics, culture, and politics.

As much as this book aims to be accessible and practical in its general survey of film theory, there are also limitations to its approach. In addition to the partial overlap between Chapters 1 and 2, there are inevitably moments that break the sequential order. In some cases, certain materials were not immediately available or were distorted by different historical contingencies. Our understanding of many theorists, for instance Kracauer, has changed significantly as additional material has become available to Anglophone readers. I consider all available materials whenever possible while also maintaining a semblance of continuity. In other cases, certain exceptions are made as a matter of other organizational parameters. For example, Chapter 1 is divided into sub-sections that focus on different national contexts (e.g. France, Germany, Soviet Russia). Here each section maintains its own chronology even though there are several points of overlap between them. Another limitation here is that, even though there is an effort to be as comprehensive as possible, it should be clear to readers that this account focuses on film theory from an Anglo-American perspective, meaning that it is devoted largely to Western European and American theorists while neglecting the many others that fall outside of that tradition. These caveats simply mean that there are many instances in which additional reading or research will be necessary or at least highly recommended to fully appreciate the entire field of film theory.

In addition to its overview approach, there are several features designed to further orient newcomers, and to optimize the book's utility for all readers. Words printed in **bold** can be found in the book's first appendix, a glossary of theoretical terms. Proper names that are both italicized and in bold—for example, ***André Bazin***—can be found in the book's second appendix, a glossary of key theorists. These resources allow students to key in on the fundamental concepts and figures within film theory, and to quickly access concise definitions and basic descriptions. While the terms and highlighted theorists in the first half of the book are fairly straightforward, these selections in the second half leave some room for debate. As film theory progresses, it is increasingly difficult to acknowledge every theorist or to clearly distinguish what should be counted as a major contribution. For this reason, some theorists are singled out for fuller discussion while others are merely mentioned in passing. These distinctions are made with some consideration for the theorist's overall contribution to the field and relevance within the immediate discussion, but, ultimately, such things are rather arbitrary and should not be taken to represent a definitive consensus.

Each chapter concludes with a series of brief discussion questions. These are designed to both reinforce the main issues covered in the chapter and encourage further consideration of certain problems or debates. These questions may also help instructors facilitate classroom discussion or coordinate supplemental reading assignments. These features aim to supplement the narrative account provided in the chapters that follow, and are a way to acknowledge that film theory extends beyond the basics covered here. This book is meant to impart readers with a narrative overview of film theory's main elements, but it should also be clear that this is an incredibly rich and expansive field that requires further consideration. Film theory offers great insight into the social, cultural, and intellectual history of the twentieth century, but fully grasping these complexities demands much more than can be provided here.

THEORY BEFORE THEORY, 1915–60

Film theory began to take shape over the first half of the twentieth century as an informal practice among individual writers, filmmakers, and enthusiasts dedicated to the new medium and its distinctive features. Although there was no formal framework or guidelines for these efforts, these early theorists did share several common aims. First and foremost, they participated in a broader effort to legitimize film. At this time, there was an overriding assumption that film did not warrant serious attention—that its popular appeal and its commercial and technological foundations necessarily meant it was antithetical to art or culture in its proper sense. To combat these general assumptions, early theorists made different claims on behalf of film's artistic merits, typically by comparing or contrasting it with existing aesthetic practices such as theater. This also involved various attempts to identify film's fundamental qualities—the formal and technical attributes that distinguished it as a medium and the practices to which it was attuned and that were necessary to advance its aesthetic potential.

The efforts of early theorists were often tied to the emergence of film connoisseurship and, by extension, the grassroots clubs, networks, and film-focused publications that were springing up in

cosmopolitan hubs across the globe. These groups were characterized by their exuberance for the new medium. They recognized
right away film's affinity for modern life and the new artistic possibilities it presented. In expounding these merits, they helped to
develop more sophisticated ways of expressing an appreciation for
its distinctive features. In this regard, the emergence of film culture provided an important foundation for elevating cinema both
aesthetically and intellectually. In France, in particular, film culture
was tied to new venues for writing about, viewing, and discussing
films. These venues eventually fostered new forms of filmmaking as
select theorists sought additional ways to augment and further articu-
late cinema's key characteristics. There was, as a result, a tendency
for theory and practice to blend together throughout this period.
Finally, this context served to establish a culture of lively debate and
ongoing exchange, one in which writers became increasingly self-
conscious of their ability to identify a canon of key films, filmmakers, distinctive performers, and genres.

At the same time that early theorists were linked in their effort to
establish the new medium's legitimacy and in their affiliation with
a growing culture of film appreciation, there were also numerous
challenges that impeded the coherence of early film theory. Some
of these were tied to the fact that film was still a new invention
and many of its formal practices were still evolving. Even with the
Hollywood system in place by 1916, new technologies like sound
and color stock required ongoing adjustments to its visual and narrative conventions. Another more pressing factor was the social,
political, and economic turmoil that persisted throughout much of
the first half of the twentieth century. Major crises in Europe not
only hindered the continent's nascent film industries—thus assur-
ing Hollywood's ascent as the leading force in filmmaking—but
in many instances disrupted the efforts of individual intellectuals,
filmmakers, and the burgeoning grassroots networks that were still
forming. Despite these challenges, the field's pioneering figures still
managed to establish a body of writing and a series of key debates
that became the foundation upon which later generations would
develop theory into an important, academically rigorous, intellectual discourse.

EARLY AMERICAN THEORISTS AND THE QUEST FOR LEGITIMACY

The publication of two books marks the official beginning of film theory. First, the poet *Vachel Lindsay* provided an inaugural attempt to cast film as an important aesthetic endeavor in his 1915 account, *The Art of the Moving Picture*. One year later, *Hugo Münsterberg* followed suit with *The Photoplay: A Psychological Study*, also arguing that film presented a unique aesthetic undertaking. In both cases, simply writing about film was a statement unto itself—an implicit attempt to elevate the medium and an argument that it warranted serious consideration despite assumptions to the contrary. The two authors shared several additional similarities. Both, for instance, used their reputations in other fields to confer credibility on the fledgling medium. Both identified key formal characteristics and began the work of establishing the distinct aesthetic merits of these attributes. As part of this particular task, both considered the relationship between film and theater, drawing attention to the ways that film surpassed its predecessor. While Lindsay and Münsterberg anticipate the main developments of early film theory, they are most noteworthy for their idiosyncrasies in attempting to navigate this uncharted territory.

For most of his career, Vachel Lindsay was best known as an American poet who enjoyed fleeting success in the 1910s and early 1920s. He was also a lifelong aesthete with a rather unconventional sense of purpose. For instance, after briefly attending art schools in Chicago and New York, Lindsay built his reputation by embarking on several "tramping" expeditions, crisscrossing the country on foot and by train attempting to barter his poems in exchange for room and board. With these expeditions, Lindsay forged a romanticized bond with both the common folk and with the physical landscape of America. He wanted to use these experiences to continue in the tradition of Walt Whitman and Ralph Waldo Emerson, but he was also adamant about cultivating a new and modern American aesthetic. Specifically, he envisioned a style that was more readily accessible to all, and that promised spiritual renewal as part of a utopian vision of the future.

Lindsay's unusual beliefs about art and society indicate an ambivalence; one that was further complicated by his vacillation between populist undercurrents and a more modern sensibility. By 1914 Lindsay had published his two most famous poems, "General William Booth Enters into Heaven" and "The Congo," in *Poetry* magazine. In short order, Lindsay became one of the country's most visible poets both performing on a nationwide circuit and participating in Progressive Era programs such as the Chautauqua education movement. While he had a distinctive performance style that helped establish him among middle-class audiences, his peers—academics and poets of the period—mainly dismissed his work as sentimental and insipid. Lindsay nevertheless incorporated modern elements both in content and form. He authored several odes celebrating Hollywood starlets such as Mary Pickford, Mae Marsh, and Blanche Sweet, and he introduced singing, chanting, and sound effects into his recitation. "The Congo," for instance, incorporated the syncopated rhythms of ragtime, the spontaneity of jazz, and racist caricatures drawn from blackface minstrelsy, all as part of Lindsay's effort to animate his poetry with the sounds of modern American life.

Such ploys were part of a broader synthesis that Lindsay termed "Higher Vaudeville." In other words, he was interested in producing an elevated version of the popular variety theater that appealed to the American masses. This aesthetic aim was also evident in another term he favored. "I am an adventurer in hieroglyphics," Lindsay once claimed. He would soon use the same term to describe motion pictures, adding further that with the "cartoons of [Ding] Darling, the advertisements in the back of the magazines and on the billboards and in the street-cars, the acres of photographs in the Sunday newspapers," America was growing "more hieroglyphic everyday" (*Art of the Moving Picture* 14). In moving pictures, he found the ideal extension of his personal aesthetic, the most dynamic and compelling iteration of this new and growing field of hieroglyphic arts. The main objective of *The Art of the Moving Picture* was indeed to establish the virtues of this new endeavor, and to suggest that it take a leading role in shaping modern American life.

Though Lindsay's discussion of film is highly impressionistic, he does propose three specific types of films that highlight the medium's specific qualities: the action film, the intimate film, and films of splendor. For each of these three categories he designates a corollary aesthetic distinction. The action film is described as sculpture-in-motion, the intimate film as painting-in-motion, and the splendor film as architecture-in-motion. These designations were not simply a matter of genre, but rather a way to foreground the medium's specific strengths and the subject matter to which it is most attuned. For example, the action film is closely linked to the chase sequence, a formula based on editing techniques such as cross-cutting and other innovations associated with the groundbreaking work of D.W. Griffith. This type of editing endowed cinema with dynamism—a rhythmic quality, an aptitude for speed, movement, and acceleration—that appealed to modern American society. This was considered sculptural in the sense that action emphasized the constituent features of the medium—its ability to capture and manipulate spatial and temporal relations. Just as the sculptor is trained to accentuate the materiality of a given medium, Lindsay believed that film should draw into relief that which "can be done in no medium but the moving picture itself" (*Art of the Moving Picture* 72).

While Lindsay emphasized the temporal dimension that film added to traditional spatial or plastic arts, he was also careful to distinguish it from time-based practices such as poetry, music, and especially theater. The reason for this was that film had begun to elicit perfunctory analogies with these other practices. Films were being described as photoplays, theatrical performances that had merely been photographed by a motion picture camera. This term had arisen as films increased in length, and as the emerging Hollywood studio system readily looked both to popular theater and proven classics for source material. On one hand, the term conferred some legitimacy, suggesting an amalgamation between cinema and an existing art. On the other hand, this association suggested a dependency, one that would enslave cinema to reputable but unadventurous conventions while forfeiting its own aesthetic specificity. Lindsay found this to be unacceptable and, instead, argued that adaptations "must be overhauled indeed, turned inside out and upside down," so that film might better adhere to the "camera-born" opportunities fostered by the new technology (*Art of the Moving Picture* 109).

It was in these moments that film most clearly captured his notion of hieroglyphics, or rather the idea that film could communicate something more than what simply appeared before the camera. The term "hieroglyph" refers to a pictographic marking or symbol that is also part of a broader system of language—at the time, one that was primarily associated with ancient Egypt. Each figure stands for a word or idea while also encapsulating different levels of meaning or indirect associations. Lindsay discusses several examples from Griffith's *The Avenging Conscience* (1914), including the close-up of a spider as it devours a fly. This was a particularly apt example in that the spider is at once part of the scenery and a highly symbolic figure or metaphor designed to enhance the film's dramatic mood. In short, the spider is more than just a spider. It sets the tone of the scene while also evoking the macabre mood for which Edgar Allan Poe—the inspiration behind *The Avenging Conscience*—was so well known (*Art of the Moving Picture* 90). More broadly, these figures could function like individual letters or words within a film, and, in turn, these units could be combined into increasingly complex patterns of signification.

The hieroglyph signaled an important advance in the emerging grammar of narrative cinema, but for Lindsay, it was also a sign of something far more decisive, a turning point in history. "The invention of the photoplay is as great a step as was the beginning of picture-writing in the stone age," he wrote (*Art of the Moving Picture* 116). And America was poised to "think in pictures," continuing the pursuit of cultural enlightenment that had been inaugurated by the Egyptians, the first "great picture-writing people" (*Art of the Moving Picture* 124, 117). This suggests that hieroglyphs might supplant language altogether, and Lindsay was adamant that the medium could serve as a universal visual language, or Esperanto, that was accessible to all. In this regard, he also believed that film was destined for an even higher calling. He proclaimed that it had the power to kindle spiritual renewal, and to nurture prophetic visions that would guide viewers to a utopian promised land. Such references made it easy for many to dismiss Lindsay as naïvely mystical, or merely eccentric. But this evangelical zeal was also an integral part of his personality, a necessary asset for someone pioneering the entirely new and still unknown field of film theory.

Just as Lindsay is better known as a poet, Hugo Münsterberg is known primarily for his work in the field of psychology. While his 1916 account *The Photoplay: A Psychological Study* is certainly more scholastic in its overall composition, its overall impact is in many ways just as peculiar as Lindsay's contribution. Münsterberg was born and educated in Germany, and he accepted a permanent faculty position at Harvard in 1897 after he was unable to secure a sufficiently prominent position in his home country. Münsterberg was appointed Professor of Experimental Psychology in Harvard's Department of Philosophy at a time when psychology was still an emerging academic discipline. His work was particularly noteworthy for his commitment to empirical data collected through scientific experimentation. Once at Harvard, he immediately set up and became the director of a modern research laboratory, which contributed significantly to both his and his department's overall reputation. Throughout his early career Münsterberg published prolifically. In addition to authoring several books devoted to his core research interests, he wrote about the psychology of litigious testimony, optimizing workplace performance, current social debates, and the relationship between Germany and America. At times, his forays into these more general topics embroiled him in controversy. This was exacerbated by his obstinate allegiance to Germany in the lead-up to World War I. At this time Münsterberg seemed to intentionally provoke his Harvard colleagues, and he was eventually accused of being a German spy.

Münsterberg completed *The Photoplay* after he had fallen into disrepute and just months before he died in 1916. The book was a strange turn in what was already an unconventional career. For his entire life, Münsterberg had rejected the movies as an undignified commercial art. He claimed that he began a "rapid conversion" after deciding on a whim to see *Neptune's Daughter*, a 1914 fantasy film starring the one-time professional swimmer Annette Kellerman (*Hugo Münsterberg on Film* 172). Some suspect that his turn to motion pictures may have been a calculated effort to repair his reputation and endear the American public that had recently censured him. The fact that it was both his final book and the only one to address the topic of film makes it difficult to fully situate in relationship to his earlier work. Still, the most striking assertion in *The Photoplay* is undoubtedly Münsterberg's contention that several cinematic techniques resemble specific cognitive procedures.

For example, he argues that the close-up—a shot in which the camera magnifies or increases the scale of a particular detail—parallels the "mental act of attention," the process by which we selectively concentrate on one aspect within a given field of sensory data. By heightening "the vividness of that on which our mind is concentrated," he explains, it is as if the close-up "were woven into our mind and were shaped not through its own laws but by the acts of our attention" (*Hugo Münsterberg on Film* 88). In other words, the film formally replicates our mental faculties. This was also evident in the "cut-back," or what became more commonly known as the flashback. In terms of narrative, a flashback is used to present an event out of chronological order. In the same way that editing allows film-makers to alternate between different locations (i.e., cross-cutting), it is also possible to shift between different moments in time (e.g. cutting from a scene in an adult character's life to an event that took place during their childhood). For Münsterberg, this technique further extends his point about the close-up: the flashback parallels the "mental act of remembering" (*Hugo Münsterberg on Film* 90). In both cases, it is again as if the "photoplay obeys the laws of the mind rather than those of the outer world" (*Hugo Münsterberg on Film* 91). The larger significance of these parallels is that they confirm the active role of cognitive faculties in shaping the cinematic experience. This upheld Münsterberg's wider-ranging interests concerning the nature of psychology. This parallel has additionally been cited as a forerunner to later film-mind analogies in developments ranging from psychoanalytic accounts of spectatorship to the rise of cognitive film theories in the 1990s.[1]

Like Lindsay, Münsterberg's account helps to identify the basic formal techniques that were integral in developing film's stylistic conventions and expressive capacity. In addition to noting their psychological dimension, Münsterberg commented on how both the close-up and the flashback elicit a strong emotional connection with viewers. The close-up, for instance, tends to focus on an actor's facial features, "with its tensions around the mouth, with its play of the eye, with its cast of the forehead, and even with the motions of the nostrils and the setting of the jaw" (*Hugo Münsterberg on Film* 99). The enlargement of such details not only heightens the psychological impact of what is shown, but also serves as part of a syntactic configuration (i.e., the arrangement of individual shots to convey a larger unit of meaning). In an earlier discussion, Münsterberg poses a hypothetical example in which "a clerk buys a newspaper on the street, glances at it and is shocked. Suddenly we see that piece of news with our own eyes. The close-up magnifies the headlines of the paper so that they fill the whole screen" (*Hugo Münsterberg on Film* 88). In this example, the close-up produces an approximation of what the character sees within the story world. This shot/reverse-shot formula was part of a broader editing strategy that helped to advance the story by linking the viewer to the point-of-view of a character. To use the language of subsequent film theorists, it serves to interpellate the viewer into the narrative and engender a sense of sympathy or identification. Flashbacks are able to mobilize this same principle. In these instances, the viewer is privy to what that character thinks about, imagines, or remembers. These particular formal devices provide evidence that narrative film possessed a unique ability to engage viewers through a series of complex psychological exchanges.

Part II of *The Photoplay* turns its attention rather exclusively to making a case for film's aesthetic legitimacy. The purpose of art, for Münsterberg, was to be autonomous—transcendental by virtue of being entirely divorced from the world. Or, as he elaborated it, "To remold nature and life so that it offers such complete harmony in itself that it does not point beyond its own limits but is an ultimate unity through the harmony of its parts, this is the aim of the isolation which the artist alone achieves" (*Hugo Münsterberg on Film* 119). This posed something of a conundrum considering the technological basis of film and the verisimilitude that was a perpetual reminder of its link to reality. Münsterberg, as a result, downplayed the medium's intrinsic capacity for mimesis. This was consistent with a tendency by many early theorists to disavow film's technological basis both because technology was the source of film's initial novelty and because the instrumental logic of modern machinery seemed to foreclose the possibility of artistic intervention. To this end, Münsterberg foregrounds not only the techniques associated with film's psychological implications, but also the medium's overarching formal configuration. Despite its realistic appearances, for example, film presents an unusual visual perspective that combines the flatness of two-dimensional images with the depth and dynamism of three-dimensionality. As he puts it, "we are fully conscious of the depth [evident within the image], and yet we don't take it for real depth" (*Hugo Münsterberg on Film* 69). This conflict is far from detrimental. On the contrary, it is what differentiates art from mere imitation. And, as Münsterberg further elaborates:

> [Film's] central aesthetic value is directly opposed to the spirit of imitation. A work of art may and must start from something which awakens in us the interests of reality and which contains traits of reality, and to that extent it cannot avoid some imitation. But *it becomes art just in so far as it overcomes reality, stops imitating and leaves the imitated reality behind it.* It is artistic just in so far as it does not imitate reality but changes the world, and is, through this, truly creative. To imitate the world is a mechanical process; to transform the world so that it becomes a thing of beauty is the purpose of art. The highest art may be furthest removed from reality.
>
> (*Hugo Münsterberg on Film* 114–15)

Münsterberg's emphasis on the use of formal devices as the basis of film's aesthetic potential anticipates subsequent theorists such as **Rudolf Arnheim** and what has more broadly been termed the **medium specificity** thesis. Writing initially in the 1930s, Arnheim enumerated a detailed catalog of the techniques that differentiate film from mere imitation. For example, he discusses composition (i.e., the use of framing, scaling, lighting, and depth of field), editing, and special effects (e.g. slow motion, superimposition, fades, and dissolves). Arnheim celebrates these tools as the necessary means for creative intervention and for developing a poetic language that belonged exclusively to film. These tools, as he explains further, "sharpen" what appears before the camera, "impose a style upon it, point out special features, make it vivid and decorative" (*Film as Art* 57). In terms that closely echo Münsterberg, art according to Arnheim "begins where mechanical reproduction leaves off, where the conditions of representation serve in some way to mold the object" (*Film as Art* 57). This type of emphasis later became known as **formalism**, the belief that film's formal practices are its defining or essential feature, one that should take precedence over all other aspects of the medium. Formalism is primarily held in opposition to **realism**, the presumption that film's verisimilitude should be its defining feature. This division became more entrenched as Arnheim adamantly rejected new sound technologies and the wider availability of color stocks, both of which promised to make film more realistic.

The ensuing debate between formalism and realism recalls the fact that new forms of art, especially those with some type of technological element, typically give rise to competing claims about what qualifies them as unique. As *Noël Carroll* has shown, arguments about medium specificity are usually a byproduct of historical circumstance.[2] They entail a struggle between existing aesthetic standards and a new generation willing to entertain the merits of new aesthetic practices. It is necessary for this latter group to claim legitimacy in some fashion and the easiest way to do so is to suggest that the new art form does something distinct that other forms cannot. With film, as is often the case, there were divergent claims regarding its fundamental qualities with different groups all vying to dictate which features should take precedence. Ultimately, these arguments testify to the fact that all art is a matter of invention and that medium specificity is culturally constructed through a combination of practical necessity and rhetorical posturing. In hindsight, it is easier to see that it is virtually impossible to reduce early theorists to one position or the other. And, moreover, it is impossible to equate film's merit with one property or the other. In this regard, labels like formalism and realism provide a convenient shorthand when surveying the emerging field of film theory, but are problematic if taken too far. And despite their different views, both sides contributed to the larger goal of legitimizing film as an aesthetic enterprise. Debate simply served as a convenient vehicle for adding vigor and urgency to this effort.

In the aggregate then, Lindsay, Münsterberg, and Arnheim were successful in elevating film as an aesthetic practice and in laying part of the groundwork for subsequent theoretical inquiry. Yet despite this general success, there are questions regarding their overall significance. Both Lindsay and Münsterberg's individual efforts, at different times, became peripheral. Their books fell out of print and were not widely read or circulated during film theory's later and more formative stages. Both remain better known for their accomplishments in other fields. Meanwhile, Arnheim's book was originally written in German in 1933 and then revised and republished in an abridged format in 1957, after he had moved on to a career in art history. While more widely read than Lindsay or Münsterberg, these irregularities added to the discontinuity of early film theory's reception.

Another mitigating factor was that these early theoretical works coincided with Hollywood's own efforts to legitimize itself as an industry. Some of the major studios made brief overtures to the likes of Lindsay and Münsterberg in various publicity campaigns designed to enrich the public's appreciation of the new medium. Though these efforts ended with questionable results, the film industry did have subsequent success in turning to other cultural gatekeepers including experimental university programs and the fledgling Museum of Modern Art.[3] While film was gradually becoming more accepted, the specific arguments of Lindsay, Münsterberg, and Arnheim were largely overshadowed by the persistence of film's more general critics on both sides of the ideological spectrum. Conservative critics were deeply suspicious of film and popular entertainment, claiming that such things were a threat to the moral character of the middle class in general and women, children, and immigrants more specifically. And at the other end of the spectrum, more radical critics were already concerned about the ways in which Hollywood might be used as an instrument of social control.[4]

FRANCE, FILM CULTURE, AND *PHOTOGÉNIE*

As film studies developed into an academic field, single-authored books became an important standard by which scholarly accomplishment is measured. In this respect, the monographs produced by Lindsay and Münsterberg provide a convenient starting point, an apparent antecedent to what eventually came later. It is important to remember, however, that throughout the early stages of film theory their particular approach was more of an exception than the rule. Few of the theorists considered throughout the remainder of this chapter wrote monographs devoted exclusively to film, and if they did, they often remained untranslated or otherwise unavailable to

English-speaking readers until much later. By contrast, then, much of early film theory was written in a piecemeal, ad hoc fashion as an extension of new forms of criticism, ongoing debates, and artist manifestos. Theory, throughout this stage of development, was not the product of isolated research or meticulous scholarly analysis. Instead, it was part of an expanding film culture and growing array of enthusiasts devoted to the medium and all of its possibilities.

France was at the center of this burgeoning film culture. It had played a significant role—certainly equal to the US—in the invention of cinema, and it had been the leading producer of films throughout the first decade of the twentieth century. However, the start of World War I in 1914 quickly brought France's film industry to a halt, which allowed the emerging Hollywood studio system to take its place as the international leader in production. This changing of the guard did not, however, diminish the country's enthusiasm for film, and actually may have even encouraged new forms of production and exhibition that would fortify a growing penchant for what became known as **cinephilia**, or an ardent infatuation for the new medium. This affinity for film culture was stoked by the intellectual milieu of the day and by Paris' status as an international epicenter of art and culture. In general, the country had a tradition of salons and cafés supported by a bourgeois clientele that generally privileged cultural sophistication. This tradition contributed to the status of France's capital as a hub for modern art and aesthetic experimentation. These factors helped to supply film with willing interlocutors and supportive patrons, both of whom were necessary in creating a culture of widespread appreciation and innovation.

By the 1910s, as Richard Abel has shown in great detail, Paris had established a fervent public forum devoted to film.[5] This included a broad spectrum of publishing outlets—ranging from specialized film journals and magazines to regular review columns in daily newspapers—that attracted intellectuals, writers, and aspiring artists. For example, **Louis Delluc**, the most influential film critic of this period, abandoned his academic studies to become a critic first at *Comoedia Illustré*, a weekly arts magazine, and later the editor-in-chief of *Le Film*, one of the first magazines devoted entirely to the new medium. Delluc quickly became a prominent figure, organizing ciné-clubs and encouraging other aspects of France's growing film culture. Throughout his writing, he engaged in speculative, sometimes polemical rhetoric to "provoke insight, new ideas, and action" (*French Film Theory and Criticism* 97). As with their counterparts in the United States, Delluc and others like Ricciotto Canudo were interested in establishing the aesthetic legitimacy of cinema. But whereas Lindsay and Münsterberg made their respective cases by defending film in its standard narrative format, Delluc and the early French critics took a more unconventional approach. For them, it was not about making film more respectable but about recognizing its artistic potential. This often meant challenging incipient assumptions about film and its reception.

In this regard, Hollywood cinema had a different valence for the French critics. Like Lindsay and Münsterberg, they were wary of films that used theatrical conventions to attract a more respectable and affluent audience. For them Hollywood provided a wholesale alternative as France gravitated in this direction with its *film d'art* movement. Hollywood, by contrast, appeared more modern and dynamic, more appealing to mass audiences, and more in synch with the technological basis of the new medium. Even so, however, it should also be noted that the celebration of these attributes was not the same thing as a straightforward endorsement of the entire Hollywood system. The studios were designed to produce commodities, and films were manufactured according to principles of efficiency and profitability. Early on, production companies minimized any acknowledgment of individual contributors, including actors and directors. Writers like Delluc were, by contrast, mainly interested in the directors, actors, genres, and techniques that exceeded the studio system's instrumental logic. For example, they discussed their deep fascination with individual actors such as Charlie Chaplin and Sessue Hayakawa, most famous for his role in *The Cheat* (1915). In recognizing the unique qualities of individual performers, Delluc and other French critics like him undermined the notion that films were simply composed of interchangeable parts. Moreover, their understanding that these figures demanded additional attention laid the groundwork for later theoretical endeavors and specifically identified **authorship** and stars as subjects worthy of critical analysis.

With regard to the specific interests of Delluc, the qualities associated with these figures were also a testament to the revelatory powers of cinematic technologies. Again in contrast to Lindsay and Münsterberg, early French theorists did not shy away from either the technological basis of film or its ambiguities. Delluc noted in general that film was the only truly modern art "because it is simultaneously and uniquely the offspring of both technology and human ideals" (*French Film Theory and Criticism* 94). For this reason, he added, "cinema will make us all comprehend the things of this world as well as force us to recognize ourselves" (*French Film Theory and Criticism* 139). Ricciotto Canudo noted that while film adheres to modern scientific principles, recording with a "clockwork precision" that captures the outward appearance of contemporary life, it simultaneously allows for "a lucid and vast expression of our internal life" (*French Film Theory and Criticism* 63, 293). As a result, "cinema gives us a visual analysis of such precise evidence that it cannot but vastly enrich the poetic and painterly imagination" (*French Film Theory and Criticism* 296). As these brief snippets suggest, it was common to juxtapose the technological components of film with the medium's aesthetic capacity while also conceding that these two attributes were inextricably intertwined. These contradictions were also evident in various elaborations of ***photogénie***, the conceptual centerpiece that tied France's early film culture together. Finally, these debates anticipated the transition from critical assessment to creative participation. While early French critics clearly admired Hollywood cinema, they were not content to be mere consumers. As such, they quickly began to appropriate Hollywood's stylistic innovations for the purpose of fostering their own alternative forms of filmmaking.

Delluc went on to write and direct six films before his death in 1924 at the age of only thirty-three. He was followed by other key figures including **Germaine Dulac** and **Jean Epstein**. Dulac, who started her career writing for early feminist magazines, introduced the term "impressionism" to describe the cinematic style that would prevail as French critics began pursuing more creative outlets for their theoretical interests. Impressionism denoted a strong interest in using film techniques to explore the porous boundaries between interior life and exterior reality. As Dulac put it, the "cinema is marvelously equipped" to express dreams, memories, thought, and emotion (*French Film Theory and Criticism* 310). She specifically identified superimposition (i.e., the combination or overlap of two distinct images) as one way of rendering an internal process that would otherwise remain imperceptible. David Bordwell has further detailed how impressionist filmmakers used formal devices to indicate a character's state of mind. Optical devices, he observes, were especially important in representing "purely mental images (e.g. a fantasy), affective states (e.g. gauze-focus over a character's wistful expression), or optically subjective states (e.g. weeping, blindness)" (*French Impressionist Cinema* 145). The use of such devices to express psychological dimensions recalls Münsterberg's earlier account, but the French filmmakers adopted these techniques in a more self-conscious manner, and were more deliberate in using them to foreground film's specificity. It is in this respect that Dulac cites examples from her own film, *Smiling Madame Beudet* (1923), to illustrate how a film author uses techniques such as the close-up "to isolate a striking expression" and further underscore "the intimate life of people or things" (*French Film Theory and Criticism* 310).

The emergence of impressionism coincided with the rise of **surrealism**, an important inter-war **avant-garde** movement, and its more experimental forays into film production. Art throughout the end of the nineteenth century had given rise to a succession of new and innovative styles that challenged existing aesthetic conventions. These practices are exemplified by movements such as Cubism and in the literary experiments of James Joyce and Gertrude Stein. While these practices are often classified under the umbrella term of **modernism**, the term "avant-garde" more specifically refers to a self-defined group, or vanguard, formed explicitly to take a lead position in cultivating new artistic possibilities. The Italian Futurists and the Dadaists, first in Zurich and later in Berlin, were among the first major avant-garde groups of the early twentieth century. Both movements have been described as a kind of anti-art, combining a penchant for anarchy with a rejection of traditional aesthetic practices. Following in the wake of these earlier groups, ***André Breton*** authored the first Surrealist Manifesto in 1924, calling more specifically for a turn to the intractable threshold between dream and reality.

In Paris, Breton assembled a group of likeminded artists, mainly writers and poets, and together issued a series of publications that explored unconventional topics ranging from occultism and madness to chance encounters. The Surrealists were especially interested in the new psychological theories developed by **Sigmund Freud**. Breton even attributed his inspiration for surrealism to a dream in which, "There is a man cut in two by the window."[6] This is as apt and elegant a description of psychoanalysis as anything. The Surrealists also had a strong interest in images and the juxtaposition of visual materials, especially through techniques such as collage and photomontage. Although Surrealism had had a strong literary focus, these interests lent themselves to cinematic experimentation and the 1920s became one of the most fertile periods in terms of avant-garde cinema. Major works included the non-narrative, abstract films of Man Ray, *Ballet méchanique* (1924) by Fernand Léger and Dudley Murphy, and René Clair's *Entr'acte* (1924). These efforts culminated with the production of *Un Chien andalou* (1929), a collaboration by Luis Buñuel and Salvador Dalí. The film uses shock to challenge bourgeois sensibilities, while also combining standard editing conventions with the imagery of unconscious desire to create a rich and provocative dream-like logic.

There was a certain amount of overlap between the Surrealists and France's still nascent film culture. Buñuel, for instance, briefly worked as an assistant on Jean Epstein's *The Fall of the House of Usher* (1928). Germaine Dulac meanwhile worked with Antonin Artaud on *The Seashell and the Clergyman* (1928), which the Surrealists subsequently attacked for its supposed insufficiencies. Despite these occasional clashes, there were also clear commonalities in their work, *photogénie* being the best-known and most interesting point of intersection. The term originated in the 1830s in conjunction with the invention of photography, literally referring to the use of light as part of the creative process but more broadly signaling "a thing or a scene lending itself well to photographic capture" (*Jean Epstein* 25). Louis Delluc rediscovered the term as part of his writing in 1919 and it quickly became a ubiquitous slogan used throughout French film culture to distinguish cinema's unique revelatory and transformative powers. The idea dovetailed with what the Surrealists found most interesting about the new medium. For example, surrealist poet Louis Aragon anticipated the main crux of *photogénie* in 1918, claiming that film endowed objects with a poetic value, transforming the prosaic into something menacing or enigmatic.[7] Throughout the 1920s, Epstein quickly became a central figure both in terms of his theoretical contributions and as an important filmmaker, in effect taking up the role originated by Delluc. In his essay "On Certain Characteristics of Photogénie," Epstein elaborates how "filmic reproduction" enhances certain things, imbuing them with "personality" or a "spirit" that otherwise remains "alien to the human sensibility" (*French Film Theory and Criticism* 314, 317). He further adds that film is a poetic medium with the capacity to reveal a new kind of reality: "the untrue, the unreal, the 'surreal'" (*French Film Theory and Criticism* 318).

Beyond the rhetorical parallels, there was a common goal within these accounts of *photogénie*. As Aragon noted, film had the power to make common objects appear strange and unfamiliar. This was consistent with the practice known as **defamiliarization**, one of the most common tactics adopted by various artists and avant-garde groups throughout this period. This could be used to evoke a sense of wonder, something beyond rational logic, and it could also be used to force viewers to question the nature of everyday existence and the relationships that allow reality to appear matter-of-fact. These objectives are also evident in Epstein's account of "Magnification," or the close-up, which he ordained the "soul of cinema" and the device that most clearly epitomized *photogénie* (*French Film Theory and Criticism* 236). In a highly lyrical excursion, he offers the following description:

> Muscular preambles ripple beneath the skin. Shadows shift, tremble, hesitate. Something is being decided. A breeze of emotion underlines the mouth with clouds. The orography of the face vacillates. Seismic shocks begin. Capillary wrinkles try to split the fault. A wave carries them away. Crescendo. A muscle bridles. The lip is laced with tics like a theater curtain. Everything is movement, imbalance, crisis. Crack. The mouth gives way, like a ripe fruit splitting open. As if slit by a scalpel, a keyboard-like smile cuts laterally into the corner of the lips.
>
> (*French Film Theory and Criticism* 235–36)

Epstein's enamored tribute to the close-up of a mouth as it begins to smile redoubles film's formal powers. His poetic language makes the object he describes strange and unusual, nearly indecipherable, but in doing so he also foregrounds the bewitching microscopic details of human physiognomy, transforming an otherwise mundane and entirely unremarkable action into something uncanny and enchanting.

Hungarian theorist and contemporary **Béla Balázs** celebrated the close-up in similar terms. He was likewise fascinated with film's ability to capture facial expression in new and unprecedented ways. Balázs further noted that while film techniques may initially intensify feelings of estrangement and alienation, they were part of a new visual culture that promised to render legible the hidden life of things including the inner experiences that had been muted by much of modern society.

Though far removed from the more combative efforts of avant-garde groups like the Surrealists, Rudolf Arnheim also acknowledged defamiliarization as an important formal device, a part of film's basic language. Citing the shot from René Clair's *Entr'acte*, in which the camera records a ballet dancer while positioned beneath a glass panel, he writes, "The strangeness and unexpectedness of this view have the effect of a clever *coup d'esprit* ('to get a fresh angle on a thing'), it brings out the unfamiliar in a familiar object" (*Film as Art* 39). For Arnheim, this produces a purely visual or aesthetic pleasure, a "pictorial surprise" for its own sake, "divorced from all meaning" (*Film as Art* 40). For later commentators, this approach placed too much emphasis on aesthetics while ignoring film's other social dimensions. As a matter of association, the French writers and filmmakers of the 1920s were likewise considered naïvely romantic in aestheticizing the new medium, particularly in the way that they endowed it with an almost mystical aura while seemingly fetishizing expressive qualities like *photogénie.*

As a result, the importance of the French theorists of the 1920s has in many respects been unfairly diminished. Later scholars did not take them seriously since they were merely enthusiasts writing in a fragmentary, and often inchoate, journalistic manner. They were further dismissed for lacking theoretical rigor or a sufficiently critical perspective. The efforts of contemporary film scholars like Richard Abel have begun the process of rediscovery and renewed engagement. For instance, there are now newly translated materials by Jean Epstein, as well as a number of recent scholarly accounts that reassess his theoretical scope and sophistication.[8] This larger project will undoubtedly shed new light on this period and its overall contribution to film theory. For the time being, however, it should be clear that France's film culture of the 1920s was more than just a mere celebration of cinema's potential. The increased interest in film was closely tied to the appearance of new outlets for writing about film, new venues for screening and debating individual films, and new alternative means of production. These developments were an important pre-condition for the later expansion of theory. They were also evidence of a new cultural vanguard deeply invested in film and its ability to produce new ways of thinking about art and modern society.

SOVIET RUSSIA AND MONTAGE THEORY

World War I had devastating consequences for all of Europe, but its most dramatic impact may have been in Russia, the country that in 1917 was swept up in a tumultuous revolution and subsequent civil war. Compared to the rest of Europe, Russia was an unlikely candidate for such a drastic transformation. The country was largely rural with a disproportionate number of uneducated peasants, it had yet to embrace full-scale industrialization, and the autocratic government, still in the hands of Tsar Nicholas II, suggested a rigid hierarchy resistant to change. Nonetheless, the combination of World War I, which had quickly descended into a horrific stalemate, and inadequate material conditions at home prompted a revolutionary vanguard, led by Vladimir Lenin and the Bolsheviks, to seize control of St. Petersburg and establish the first Communist government. The immediate aftermath was chaotic and acrimonious, but also steeped in a certain sense of exhilaration. The prospect of creating a new society, embracing technology and modern principles for the betterment of all, and pioneering a new political model brought the promise of excitement and innovation. It was this excitement that was at the center of Soviet Russia's embracing of cinema and its development of **montage theory**.

Like many key terms within film theory and criticism, montage is a French expression and in its main sense it refers to editing (i.e., the splicing together of individual shots). In the 1920s, however, the term took on additional distinction by virtue of its association with the leading Soviet film theorists and practitioners **Sergei Eisenstein** and **Dziga Vertov**. It not only represented an important technique for these filmmakers, but also dovetailed with the ideological underpinnings of the Revolution and with broader artistic and intellectual interests of the time. From a political standpoint, the Communist Revolution had been inspired by the ideas of **Karl Marx**, one of the most important and influential thinkers of the modern era. Though Marx was a trained philosopher, he was drawn to politics and soon became involved in various socialist and workers' movements. In 1848, amidst widespread revolutionary ferment throughout the industrialized cities of Europe, Marx co-authored the *Communist Manifesto* with his frequent collaborator Frederick Engels. In it, Marx and Engels warn that a specter haunts Europe, the specter of radical social change in which the working class or proletariat rise up to demolish the existing hierarchy. Both in the manifesto and throughout his later, more sustained theoretical work, Marx aimed to raise class consciousness by encouraging the proletariat to reclaim the labor that had been systematically alienated from them—extracted for the sole purpose of maintaining a system of inequality and dehumanizing exploitation.

Amidst the transition that followed the Revolution, Lenin endorsed film as an important instrument for the new Soviet state. In 1919, the film industry was nationalized and placed under the direction of Narkompros, the new state-run ministry of culture. That same year, the Moscow Film School or All-Union State Institute of Cinematography (abbreviated as VGIK) was established. It was meant to serve primarily as a training facility, but due to the severe shortage of film stock and other equipment at the time, it was necessary to explore other types of curriculum. **Lev Kuleshov**, a fledgling director who began working in the pre-revolutionary period, set up a workshop in association with the school where he and his students began exploring the formal structure of film and the innovative uses of editing in American films like Griffith's *Intolerance* (1916). For Kuleshov, "the essence of cinematography" was without question a matter of editing. "[W]hat is important is not what is shot in a given piece," he explained, "but how the pieces in a film succeed one another, how they are structured" (*Kuleshov On Film* 129). Ultimately, the workshop became best known for an experiment labeled the "Kuleshov effect." By editing the same initial shot together with several different reverse shots, the experiment suggested that an actor's appearance is determined less by his facial expression than by what he is looking at. Kuleshov's investigations quickly became the foundation for an ensuing generation of Soviet filmmakers, and editing became the primary means by which they sought to advance the new medium.

As a practical technique, editing also resonated with elements of Marx's conceptual framework. His theoretical method is sometimes referred to as **dialectical materialism**, a combination of Hegelian dialectics and his own account of economic determinism in which material conditions determine one's social class. Marx believed that class struggle, and more specifically the conflict between opposing class interests, was the engine that would move history forward. Eisenstein, while often fast and loose in his interpretations of Marx, was the most explicit in his efforts to introduce a dialectical approach to film form. As he bluntly put it, "montage is conflict" (*Eisenstein Reader* 88). While art in general aimed to forge new concepts through "the dynamic clash of opposing passions" (*Eisenstein Reader* 93), editing allowed for the ongoing juxtaposition of individual shots. In this regard, editing promised to serve in a dialectical manner. It was tantamount to smashing film's basic material units—the individual shot—apart to generate something like the "explosions of the internal combustion engine" (*Eisenstein Reader* 88). Film form would act as a catalyst, a kind of fuel that was necessary to ensure intellectual and historical progress.

The turn to editing was not only a matter of revolutionary rhetoric but also part of a broader zeitgeist that extended to art and intellectual circles that had existed prior to the events of 1917. The Russian Futurists were a loosely formed avant-garde group intrigued by the dynamism of industrial modernity, especially its speed and complexity. This group included key figures like Kazimir Malevich, Vsevolod Meyerhold, and Vladimir Mayakovsky, working in different media—painting, theater, and poetry, respectively. After the Revolution these artists, joined by Alexander Rodchenko and El Lissitzky—both of whom specialized in photography and graphic design—pioneered a new movement known as constructivism. One of its main principles was that artists should serve as a new type of engineer capable of using scientific techniques to construct "socially useful art objects—objects that would enhance everyday life" (*Art into Life* 169). Their slogan "art into life" carried the broader belief that the Revolution had set the stage for an entirely new and egalitarian society, one in which art would play a practical role. At the same time, the exact manner in which this was to take place was a matter of contentious debate. As in France, various factions within this group issued polemical manifestos, often attacking one another and engendering intense debate within the pages of *LEF*, the journal of the Left Front of the Arts, and other avant-garde publications.

Soviet montage theory was also influenced by the contemporaneous emergence of the **Russian Formalists**, an informal network of intellectuals and scholars that included groups such as the Moscow Linguistic Circle and the Society for the Study of Poetic Language in St. Petersburg. The Formalists shared an interest in language and were inspired by the developing science of modern linguistics. In the same way that linguistics focused its attention on the basic units of language, the Formalists attempted to critically engage the basic units of literature. They drew, for example, a distinction between *fabula* and *syuzhet*. The former refers to the chronological order of events, or **story**. The latter refers to the actual arrangement of these events, or **plot**.[9] This distinction allowed for a more precise interrogation of the relationship between form and content, and established how literature, as well as film, functioned as a multi-dimensional textual system.

In addition to their interest in specific structural elements, the Formalists proposed a broader theory of art. According to Victor Shklovsky, one of the most prominent members of this group, art should produce knowledge by "enstranging objects and complicating form" (*Theory of Prose* 6). As life becomes habitual and routine, we are no longer able to see things as they really are. Art provides the devices that are necessary for us to see these things anew. Shklovsky's notion of *ostranenie*, the Russian term for "making strange," clearly resonated with the French avant-garde's use of defamiliarization. This term also became closely associated with alienation effects, a technique later developed by German playwright ***Bertolt Brecht***. Such sentiments were also evident in various accounts of montage. Dziga Vertov, for instance, argued that Kino-Eye (i.e., the umbrella term he used to describe his style of filmmaking) should be used to make "the invisible visible, the unclear clear, the hidden manifest, the disguised overt," all as part of a coordinated effort to transform "falsehood into truth" (*Kino-Eye* 41). While defamiliarization indicates an important parallel between the Russian Formalists and Soviet filmmakers, there were also notable variations. Most significantly, the Russian Formalists were part of a larger undertaking they termed **poetics**. This refers to a form of literary analysis that examines particular texts to extrapolate their governing formal properties. Their growing interest in this type of analysis marked a departure from the group's earlier affinity for avant-garde techniques and has served as a point of reference for subsequent movements ranging from American New Criticism to structuralism. More recently, film scholars like David Bordwell and Kristin Thompson have reclaimed poetics as part of their neoformalist approach.[10]

These different influences are all apparent in the work of Eisenstein, the director and theorist who quickly emerged as the leading figure in Soviet cinema. While briefly serving with the Red Army, Eisenstein began working in theater. After the civil war he continued to pursue this as a professional career, first as a set designer at the Proletkult Theater in Moscow and then as a director. Between 1920 and 1924, Eisenstein studied both with the constructivist director Vsevolod Meyerhold and with the Petersburg-based Factory of the Eccentric Actor or FEKS. This experimental group specifically embraced "low arts" like the cabaret, fairground amusements, and cinema as a way "to attack the hegemony of 'high' art" (*Film Factory* 21). It was at this time that Eisenstein developed his notion of the **attraction**, an aggressive device "calculated to produce specific emotional shocks in the spectator" (*Eisenstein Reader* 30). He further advocated for a combination, or montage, of these devices. In his first full stage production, for instance, Eisenstein created a circus-like atmosphere, incorporating clowns and acrobats to emphasize kinesis and to challenge traditional notions of set construction. The play was also infamous for its grand finale. According to Eisenstein, fireworks were placed beneath each seat in the auditorium and set to explode just as the play came to an end. In this regard, the attraction was designed to agitate the audience through a combination of cerebral and sensory provocations. This was meant not only to physically incite spectators, but also to attune them to the force necessary to overcome the inertia of existing ideological structures.

As Eisenstein moved on to film production—completing his first film, *Strike*, in 1924—he argued that the attraction would continue to serve as an important tactic. For example, he described the final sequence of *Strike* as an "attractional schema" (*Eisenstein Reader* 39). The film concludes with a scene that cuts between images of fallen workers and the slaughter of a bull. This was designed to emphasize the "bloody horror" of the workers' defeat (*Eisenstein Reader* 38). In this regard, the attraction is both a precursor and transition to Eisenstein's more elaborate theories of montage as a strictly cinematic technique. In terms of his example from *Strike*, he says that the intercutting engenders a "thematic effect," producing an association or correspondence that ultimately amounts to something more than the sum of its parts (*Eisenstein Reader* 38). Eisenstein subsequently developed this notion in reference to hieroglyphs and other written characters. In the essay "Beyond the Shot," he compares the juxtaposition of individual film shots to how Japanese ideograms combine specific graphic references to produce abstract concepts. In this same essay, Eisenstein takes a stronger rhetorical position by claiming that these individual parts are not simply interlocking units but rather an occasion for engendering dialectical opposition. In developing this position, he further amplified the aggressive aspects of the attraction, going so far as to compare his style of montage to a fist. It was in this capacity that montage was intended to pummel the audience with a "series of blows" (*Eisenstein Reader* 35).

While Eisenstein made montage the cornerstone of both his theoretical and practical approach to film, he was also relatively elastic in adapting and expanding his exact methods. As part of his effort to emphasize conflict, for example, he recognized that other formal elements could be just as important as editing and the simple relationship between individual shots. In his second film *Battleship Potempkin* (1925), Eisenstein used staging and graphic counterpoints within the mise-en-scene, most famously in the climactic "Odessa Steps" sequence, to sensational effect. In a 1928 statement co-authored with Vsevolod Pudovkin and Grigori Alexandrov, Eisenstein expressed his interest in sound cinema. Though he understood that this new technology would be predominantly used to create the illusion of synchronicity, he also believed that as a new formal element sound could be used to create discord. It could thus be used to further enhance the principles of montage.[11] As Eisenstein expanded his understanding of montage, he also began exploring more abstract variations on his earlier, more materially focused, dialectical approach. It was at this point that he introduced new categories such as tonal and overtonal to his more standard notions of montage based on acceleration, alternation, and rhythmic calculation. Tonal montage refers to scenes organized around a dominant thematic or emotional motif—as in the conclusion to *Strike*. In terms of introducing multiple themes or ideas, these could be juxtaposed over the course of a sequence to produce additional, conceptual overtones. In certain cases, these overtones could be further coordinated to engender a more complex association in what Eisenstein termed intellectual montage. To illustrate, he cites a famous sequence in *October* (1928) whereby several religious idols are joined together in a montage designed to illustrate religion's hypocrisy. Although intellectual montage remained a difficult and evasive concept, it illustrates Eisenstein's effort to continually expand montage both as a formal practice and as part of a larger theoretical project.

As Eisenstein developed increasingly complex notions of montage, he continued to work within a narrative framework. This distinguished him from Dziga Vertov, the other major practitioner of montage during this time and Eisenstein's occasional rival. Vertov began working with film in 1918 as part of the state's initial campaign to tour the country with short, propagandistic newsreels that were meant to rally support for the new government. While working with his brother, cinematographer Boris Kaufman, and his wife, editor Elizaveta Svilova, Vertov developed a program that called for *Kino-pravada* or film truth. Throughout various manifestos and short writings, they collectively celebrated the camera's ability to capture and record reality. These efforts helped to pioneer a new genre known as documentary. Contemporaries like Robert Flaherty and John Grierson were exploring similar terrain, which they described as "the creative treatment of actuality."[12] While documentary emphasized film's verisimilitude, government officials in the United States, the United Kingdom, and Germany, like those in the Soviet Union, were all eager to explore the possibilities of film as a mass medium. These governments held certain notions that film would function as a public service, but their efforts often amounted to state-sponsored propaganda.

Even though Vertov maintained a fundamental allegiance to select documentary principles, he simultaneously embraced formal experimentation including the use of trick photography, optical effects, and self-reflexive commentary. These techniques were necessary to demonstrate cinema's ability to see what the human eye could not. In his 1924 film *Kino-glaz*, for example, he uses reverse motion to track the origin of a commodity, in this case the piece of meat that is being sold at a local market. In doing so, he shows the transformation that the commodity must undergo and the labor incumbent within that process. The sequence serves to defamiliarize a common commercial good while also deconstructing **commodity fetishism** more generally. In his masterpiece, *Man with a Movie Camera* (1929), Vertov cuts between several scenes of manual labor, including the assembly of textiles, and shots of his editor Svilova as she combines individual celluloid frames. This not only illustrates the formalist doctrine of laying bare the devices that underlie artistic production, but also draws attention to parallel structures of labor within industrialized society. This was another facet of Vertov's Kino-Eye. It aimed to elicit "the internal rhythm" that linked modern machinery to different forms of labor (*Kino-Eye* 8).

With the international success of *Battleship Potemkin*, Eisenstein quickly became an iconic representative of cinema's potential as a serious art. Between 1929 and 1932, his reputation continued to grow while he traveled the world as an ambassador for Soviet culture and the principles of montage. And yet even with this success, Eisenstein's actual situation was a bit more complicated. Some of his admirers in the West celebrated his cinematic accomplishments with little consideration for his political or theoretical concerns. Political dissidents and the intelligentsia meanwhile welcomed him as a comrade-in-arms but did not fully understand or appreciate his aesthetic sensibility. Many others were wary of the new Soviet experiment writ large and condemned anyone associated with it as a subversive enemy. In addition to all of this, the Soviet Union had become a very different place by the time Eisenstein returned in 1932.

The sense of exhilaration and avant-garde ferment of the 1920s quickly disappeared as Joseph Stalin rose to power. Formalism was officially denounced in favor of "socialist realism." Artists like Eisenstein and Vertov were censured, never able to work again entirely on their own terms. By the time the Soviet Union became involved in World War II, and then the Cold War, the revolutionary euphoria of the 1920s was a distant memory.

GERMANY AND THE FRANKFURT SCHOOL

As World War I came to an end, Germany, similar to the Soviet Union, was engulfed by social and political disarray. The new Weimar Republic, the parliamentary government installed in 1919 as a condition of Germany's surrender to the Allied Powers, attempted to institute democratic reforms but remained fundamentally unstable, hindered in part by the economic volatility brought on by debt and astronomical inflation. It was in this context that Felix Weil, together with the financial support of his industrialist father Herman, founded the Institute of Social Research in 1923. As a student, Weil had participated in emerging debates about Marxist principles and socialist politics, and after completing his studies he became a patron to various leftist endeavors. With the Institute, Weil sought to establish a permanent framework for conducting research and supporting scholars interested in new forms of social theory. In this regard, the Institute was designed to facilitate the types of inter-disciplinary, critical perspectives that had essentially been prohibited within the rigid confines of the official education system.

The Institute was affiliated with Frankfurt University, one of the newer and more liberal universities, but it also maintained a significant degree of intellectual and financial independence due to Weil's generous support. This ensured freedom to pursue unorthodox topics and more generally provided the resources that were necessary to conduct serious academic research. For instance, the Institute's endowment specifically provided funding for staff, library materials, and additional support for graduate students. While the **Frankfurt School** is often used as an interchangeable euphemism for the Institute itself, it also serves as a more inclusive designation. It encompasses both the Institute's multiple variations as it was forced to relocate following the Nazi's rise to power and, more importantly, it includes the intellectuals that were only nominally affiliated with the Institute. It is in this respect that **Siegfried Kracauer** and **Walter Benjamin** are considered part of the Frankfurt School. Though they shared many of the same influences and interests (ranging from the philosophy of Hegel, Kant, and Nietzsche as well as the more recent work of sociologists Georg Simmel and Max Weber), they never gained the Institute's full support. It may be because of this that they were also among the few members of the Frankfurt School to vigorously consider the theoretical implications of film.

Kracauer was deeply enmeshed in the intellectual life of Weimar Germany and he, like Benjamin, maintained personal friendships with many of the Institute's leading members. At the same time, he had taken a much more eclectic professional path than the other scholars associated with the Institute. He spent most of his life as a journalist and freelance writer. Throughout most of the 1920s he served as a regular contributor, and later as a full editor, to the cultural section in the *Frankfurter Zeitung*, one of Germany's most prominent bourgeois newspapers. The rise of the Nazis prompted Kracauer to leave for Paris in 1933, where he continued as editor for the newspaper. Throughout this period Kracauer wrote extensively about all aspects of popular culture, including film. In doing so, he developed the foundations for his later works, though this was not clear until the 1990s when his early essays were translated and more widely available.[13] Kracauer eventually gained entry to the United States in 1941 where at the age of fifty-one he reinvented himself as a film scholar. The 1947 publication of *From Caligari to Hitler*, a critical history of German cinema during the Weimar period, and *Theory of Film* in 1960 established Kracauer as one of the preeminent experts in the still developing field of film study.

At the time of its publication, *Theory of Film* was comprehensive and insightful, a deft overview of the medium and the critical debates that it had generated. Like many early theorists, however, Kracauer fell victim to the volatility of ever-changing scholarly sensibilities. As film studies began to gain ground in the late 1960s and 1970s, Kracauer was viewed as overly schematic, even pedantic. Moreover, the book's main thesis that film has an intrinsic affinity for recording and revealing reality placed Kracauer within the tradition of realism at a time when it was considered naïve if not entirely wrongheaded. It is only recently that film scholar **Miriam Hansen** has highlighted the inadequacy of these assessments. In her introduction to the most recent edition of *Theory of Film*, Hansen details how this later work is encrypted with Kracauer's earlier concerns, specifically his complex views regarding modernity and film's ability to reverse its negative impact. Hansen further notes that even amidst Kracauer's belabored organization it is difficult to avoid its more nuanced undercurrents. She points specifically to his repeated references to Marcel Proust's discussion of a photograph in *Remembrance of Things Past*. To take another example, consider a brief mention of the close-up, a captivating figure among early viewers and fledgling theorists alike. Kracauer writes that the "close-up reveals new and unsuspected formations of matter," such that "skin textures are reminiscent of aerial photographs, eyes turn into lakes or volcanic craters. Such images blow up our environment in a double sense: they enlarge it literally; and in doing so, they blast the prison of conventional reality, opening up expanses which we have explored at best in dreams before" (*Theory of Film* 48). Contrary to his detractors, the passage is rich and suggestive. More importantly, it conceptually deviates from his supposedly stolid endorsement of film's realist function.

In his brief account of the close-up, film becomes an intersection of divergent forces. It is at once organic (skin-like), technical and abstract (an aerial photograph), material (resembling natural and geological phenomena), and imaginary (dream-like). This is not entirely surprising since Kracauer had welcomed this type of dialectical entanglement throughout his early writings. It was precisely through the interplay between these opposing forces that Kracauer sharpened his critical analysis of modern life. He more broadly termed this method the "go-for-broke game of history" (*Mass Ornament* 61). This method can also be seen in his account of the **mass ornament**, a label Kracauer used to describe a new popular fashion in which individuals were assembled into larger patterns or formations. He was thinking specifically of marching demonstrations and dance troupes such as the Tiller Girls, but the phenomenon would soon also be prominently featured in film, most spectacularly in the baroque musical numbers orchestrated by Hollywood director Berkeley Busby. Kracauer starts his analysis with a harsh critique of these new configurations. In effect, they aestheticize the calculated, instrumental logic of the capitalist production process. The mass ornament, in this respect, produces a complete and pleasurable structure in which its individual parts are rendered imperceptible. This process closely parallels the manner in which the labor necessary to manufacture a commodity is obscured in the final product. "Everyone," as Kracauer notes, "does his or her task on the conveyor belt, performing a partial function without grasping the totality" (*Mass Ornament* 78).

At the same time, Kracauer was wary of simple bourgeois condemnations of popular culture and the kneejerk Marxist interpretations that dismissed such things as mere capitalist exploitation. Indeed, what distinguished Kracauer from his friends in the Institute was his willingness to engage new forms of mass culture with the same intellectual rigor that many believed was warranted only by more refined forms of culture such as literature and music. And while Kracauer ultimately preferred many of the same modernist and avant-garde practices that his peers would privilege in their analyses of modern culture, his approach differed significantly in at least one key respect. Other Frankfurt School scholars followed precursors like the Soviet montage theorists in advocating or elaborating the specific methods that were considered capable of challenging social and aesthetic conventions. Kracauer, by contrast, embraced a more dialectic form of ideology critique. He generated critical diagnoses based on his interpretation of existing culture and its various symptoms. But he also did so in a way that fully confronted both the complexity of mass culture and the potential ways in which contemporary audiences could respond to such forms.

To this end, Kracauer suggests that the "inconspicuous surface-level" expressions within mass culture cannot be taken entirely at face value even though they may simultaneously hold the key to "the fundamental substance" of things (*Mass Ornament* 75). And as a result, it is necessary to attend not only to the surface and its subterranean complement but also to the way that they "illuminate each other reciprocally" (*Mass Ornament* 75). This maneuvering allows Kracauer to revise his initial critique of the mass ornament. Though the aestheticization of industrial society does disguise its brutal realities, it also has the potential to reveal the shortcomings of the capitalist system. In particular, Kracauer suggests that the mass ornament shows how the rational logic that undergirds this system does not go far enough. Instead, it is a testament to capitalism's reliance on superficial distraction and the "mindless consumption of the ornamental patterns" to preserve traditional social hierarchies and consolidate power in the hands of a few. In his 1927 essay, "Photography," Kracauer had identified similarly paradoxical dynamics, establishing a model for both the mass ornament and his later investigation of cinema. With all three he held out hope for their revelatory potential, a hope that culminated in film's "redemption of physical reality," the telling subtitle to *Theory of Film*. This attribute, as he writes in its epilogue, was not a matter of straightforward realism but rather a facet of film's ability to render "visible what we did not, or perhaps could not, see before its advent." Film allows us to discover the material world anew, to redeem it "from its dormant state, its state of virtual nonexistence." Film helps us "to appreciate our given material environment" and to "virtually make the world our home" once again (*Theory of Film* 300).

The return to Kracauer as an important Frankfurt School theorist is a recent development. By contrast, Walter Benjamin attracted a strong following rather quickly after the English translation of his work in the 1968 collection, *Illuminations*. In fact, Benjamin has become so prominent that he is likely the best-known representative of the Frankfurt School. This is odd since he, like Kracauer, had a tenuous, and often peripheral, relationship with the Institute. His marginal status was compounded by the fact that he was never able to secure a university position despite his formal training and obvious erudition. He was, as a result, forced to cobble out a meager living as a freelance writer, often relying on the financial support of his bourgeois family. When Benjamin died in 1940, committing suicide while attempting to escape fascist Europe, he was an obscure and little-known figure.

When his work did finally become more widely available, it was his essay, "The Work of Art in the Age of Mechanical Reproduction" (alternately known by variations such as "The Work of Art in the Age of Its Technological Reproducibility"), that drew the most interest. In it, Benjamin suggests that modern technology has fundamentally changed art. Most notably, he says that its **aura** has been rendered obsolete, meaning that art has lost its sense of authenticity or singularity, and, by extension, the cult-like rituals that it once supported. In the dominant reading of the essay, Benjamin is seen as celebrating technology, with film as his primary example, as a democratic tool, capable of emancipating society from the traditional forms of power such as religion. Though this reading continues to hold sway, Miriam Hansen, as part of her overall re-evaluation of the Frankfurt School, has made an extensive and convincing case for at least a partial reassessment of this view.

Part of Benjamin's overall appeal has been his unique approach to an eclectic, and sometimes obscure, range of topics. This was evident in his first book, *The Origin of German Tragic Drama*, a work that Benjamin originally submitted as his post-doctoral thesis only to apparently bewilder his academic supervisors. As a key part of this analysis of sixteenth and seventeenth-century baroque dramaturgy, Benjamin identified allegory both as a structuring device within this period and as a method for accessing the historical undercurrents within certain cultural formations. It became an important concept throughout his larger body of work, and was the guiding principle in the never-completed Arcades Project, Benjamin's attempt to excavate a history of modern Paris through an idiosyncratic account of its shop-lined, enclosed walkways. This unique approach was equally apparent even as he engaged in more conventional topics. For instance, his "On Some Motifs in Baudelaire" quickly shifts away from poet Charles Baudelaire to a much broader consideration of the relationship between technology and modern life. While borrowing from Freud's account of shock in *Beyond the Pleasure Principle*, Benjamin suggests that we have necessarily adopted a protective shield to mitigate the sensory overload and other negative effects brought on by modern, industrialized society. As a result, it is necessary for art, in this case Baudelaire, to produce "harsh" images that are capable of reaching an audience that has otherwise grown numb to certain types of experience. Film, Benjamin adds in the same essay, is especially adept at producing these new forms of stimuli. In producing these shocks, the medium has the potential to breach the protective shield that has rendered society docile and apathetic.

What's challenging in Benjamin's account is that technology is at once the problem and a potential solution. When applied on a mass scale as part of industrialization, technology incapacitates its users. When enlisted in the service of certain types of art, it can be used to reverse technology's negative impact. In this regard, Benjamin's position resembles Kracauer's account of the mass ornament as both acutely emblematic of the capitalist system and a prescient cipher capable of revealing the limits and contradictions of that system. Benjamin further developed his paradoxical view of technology in his essay, "Little History of Photography," and, more specifically, in what he termed the **optical unconscious**. Contrary to strictly realist accounts of photography and the cinematic image, Benjamin argues that even "the most precise technology can give its products a magical value," that these mechanically produced documents bear traces of an alien "here and now," the "tiny spark of contingency" that confirms "it is another nature which speaks to the camera rather than to the eye" (*Selected Writings v. 2* 510). This "other" nature is akin to what Freud identified as the **unconscious**, a realm within human subjectivity where unfiltered desires and repressed, or socially unacceptable, thoughts are made to reside. Though Benjamin, prompted by the Surrealists' embrace of psychoanalysis, was an able reader of Freud, he was less concerned with the term as a matter of psychological doctrine than as an evocative figure. Film was capable of registering that which was omnipresent within the visible world yet somehow unseen, the "physiognomic aspects" that "dwell in the smallest things." These further encompass the fleeting details that are "meaningful yet covert enough to find a hiding place in waking dreams" (*Selected Writings v. 2* 512). In this regard, the optical unconscious was related to the avant-garde practice of defamiliarization. And yet Benjamin also found examples of the optical unconscious within contemporary cinema. Popular figures such as Charlie Chaplin and Mickey Mouse were simultaneously familiar and strange, uncanny in their ability to provide mass entertainment while also bearing witness to the barbarism inherent in industrialized modernity.

Although the dominant reading of the "Work of Art" essay emphasizes the eradication of aura as a necessary condition in the democratic enlistment of cinema, Benjamin's interest in the optical unconscious suggests a more ambivalent position. In some respects, for instance, film's ability to render certain "magical" attributes within its images comes dangerously close to reclaiming aura as an inescapable feature of the medium. Moreover, Benjamin appeared willing to complicate the idea of aura in his specific discussion of the relationship between film actors and their audience. Film, in contrast to theater, creates an irrevocable divide between the actor and the audience. Initially, Benjamin suggests that this void, and the loss of shared presence, underscores film's annihilation of aura. He goes on, however, to say that this produces a new relationship whereby actor and audience bond by virtue of their connection with the camera, the apparatus that mediates their exchange. This is made all the more interesting in that the camera is absent within the image. It is in this regard that the "equipment-free aspect of reality" that appears on screen becomes "the height of artifice" (*Selected Writings v. 4* 263). In other words, it serves as a dialectical image that contains both what is there and what is not. And in this sense it also functions allegorically, reverberating the absent relationship between actor and audience.

In most cases, the Hollywood system and its ilk simply neutralized the radical potential of these dynamics. The strange and alienating effects associated with the optical unconscious were subordinated to the commercial logic of the entertainment industry. Show business responds by building up the "personality" of its stars, creating a cult-like fascination that preserves a kind of "magic" or contrived aura in its most valuable commodities (*Selected Writings v. 4* 261). Even with this being so, Benjamin maintained the possibility that film, along with other facets of modern culture, had the potential to reshape the way we see the world and, in turn, fundamentally transform social relations. In an essay exalting the Surrealists, Benjamin linked this potential to what he designated profane illuminations. Although there were different ways of producing these transformative moments, they were to a certain extent structurally implicit within film's basic formal methods. In a passage that recalls the avant-garde ethos of Epstein and Vertov, Benjamin writes that film's arrival has "exploded this prison-world with the dynamite of the split second." This is tied to techniques such as the close-up, which expands space, bringing "to light entirely new structures of matter," and to slow motion, which discloses "unknown aspects" within familiar movements (*Selected Writings v. 4* 265–266). These techniques promise not only a "heightened presence of mind," but also a model for using new technologies as part of a larger effort to improve social conditions and catapult history forward.

Whereas Kracauer and Benjamin developed a complex series of ideas with respect to film, the Frankfurt School as a whole became closely identified with a more critical position. This is most clearly evident in the work of **Theodor Adorno**, a leading figure in the actual Institute and a major philosopher and social critic in his own right. Unlike Kracauer and Benjamin, Adorno had little hope for the new medium. On the contrary, Adorno is best known for condemning popular culture—especially popular music and jazz—while instead endorsing various modernist practices and the possibilities he associated with autonomous art. His critical views are epitomized in "The Culture Industry," an essay co-written with Max Horkheimer while both men were living in the US exiled by Nazi Germany. Throughout the essay they offer a devastating critique of film and mass culture more generally as a homogenous and fundamentally brutal facet of modern society. "Entertainment," they write, "is the prolongation of work under late capitalism. It is sought by those who want to escape the mechanized labor process so that they can cope with it again" (*Dialectic of Enlightenment* 109). In this regard, the culture industry is considered synonymous with certain sadomasochistic dynamics. Film and other forms of popular entertainment such as cartoons present viewers with images of violence that mask the violence that they themselves must accept as a condition of their work-a-day world. The laughter elicited by such cartoons serves as a form of compensation. But it is also one that further accustoms viewers to the exploitive rhythms of modern, industrialized society.

The culture industry critique was not only representative of the Frankfurt School's position but it also became the general line for many intellectuals and social critics in the years that followed World War II. The mass culture critique posited by Dwight MacDonald, and later developed by Herbert Marcuse in *One-Dimensional Man*, often coalesced into a complete rejection of mass culture. This was part of a broader turn by cultural elites away from film and popular culture. This has made for a rather contradictory legacy. The Institute provided an initial model for generating serious theoretical scholarship engaged in the rigorous analysis of culture and society. Yet, in Adorno's wholesale condemnation, the Frankfurt School appeared

to foreclose further consideration of mass culture, essentially undo-
ing much of the work that other early theorists had so diligently
undertaken. The Frankfurt School practice of Critical Theory, an
inter-disciplinary synthesis of Marxism, psychoanalysis, and ideology critique, at the same time anticipated many of the theoretical
interests that took root in post-war France. However, in 1946 the
Institute returned to Germany, largely abandoning the international
connections it had forged while in exile, and remained detached
from larger intellectual developments in the post-war period. And,
finally, Kracauer and Benjamin, two of Weimar Germany's most
original and compelling thinkers, were relegated to a secondary tier
throughout the Frankfurt School's initial reception. Despite their
incisive and diverse thoughts on cinema, the full range of their work
has only recently become available to Anglophone readers. As with
the French theorists of the 1920s, their work is currently a matter of
renewed interest.

POST-WAR FRANCE: FROM NEOREALISM TO THE NEW WAVE

The vibrant film culture that had flourished in France during the
1910s and 1920s largely came to end in the decade leading up to
World War II. The exact reasons for this are not clear though external factors like international economic depression and the rise of
political regimes hostile to modern art certainly took a toll. Other
factors, like the introduction of sound technology and internal
power struggles among avant-garde groups like the Surrealists, may
have also contributed to this decline. Regardless of which circumstances were most responsible for this decline, France's film culture
following World War II had to be reinvented anew. This task largely
fell to *André Bazin*, a perspicacious and dedicated enthusiast who
worked tirelessly in the post-war aftermath to develop a new culture
of informed criticism and sustained engagement. As part of these
efforts, Bazin inspired a younger generation of critics and fledgling
filmmakers, many of whom went on to have a dramatic impact long
after his death in 1958. Bazin also wrote extensively during this time,
mainly short articles and essays for a variety of journals and other

publications. His organizing efforts culminated with the founding of *Cahiers du cinéma*, one of the most well-regarded sources of writing on film and a major touchstone in the establishment of film study as a serious academic subject. It was here that Bazin inaugurated a decisive shift to realism and officially recognized the aesthetics that came to dominate post-WWII European art cinemas.

In the 1930s, the French film industry gave rise to a style of narrative filmmaking known as poetic realism. Directors like Jean Renoir and Marcel Carné used this style to create lyrical yet unembellished portraits of everyday, often working-class, life. While still adhering to narrative conventions, these films tended to adopt the more naturalistic aesthetics of documentary. With this style, Bazin found the basis for what he believed was film's defining feature: its ineffable bond with the social world and an ability to truthfully depict life's beauty and complexity. Unlike the montage theorists, Bazin was not interested in producing calculated effects through the manipulation of film's formal structure. Nor was he convinced, like earlier theorists Münsterberg and Arnheim, that film's most important feature lay in the limitations of its verisimilitude. To make his case to the contrary, Bazin, like Kracauer and Benjamin before him, began by turning to film's technological precursor. In his essay "The Ontology of the Photographic Image," Bazin broadly suggests that the purpose of art is to preserve life. The photograph succeeds at this task insofar as it eliminates the human component from the process. Indeed, the mechanical nature of photography satisfies our "irrational" desire for something in its original state. And to this end, Bazin infamously declared, "The photographic image is the object itself." It is not a reproduction, but rather "it *is* the model" (*What Is Cinema? v. 1* 14). The exact meaning of Bazin's assertion has been the source of tremendous consternation. Some suggest that he recognized film's **indexical** quality, a distinction established in an unrelated context by ***Charles Sanders Peirce*** to indicate signs that share an existential bond with their referent (e.g. fingerprints etc.).[14] For others, the claim was simply evidence of Bazin's errant ways: his naïve idealism, his Catholicism, and his unapologetic faith in the camera as an objective recording apparatus.

This understanding of the photographic image was the linchpin in Bazin's commitment to realism. At the same time, he extended his support to a range of practitioners and techniques that adhered more to the spirit than the letter of this commitment. In addition to Renoir, Bazin identified Erich von Stroheim, Orson Welles, Carl Theodore Dreyer, and Robert Bresson as key directors who "put their faith in reality" (*What Is Cinema? v. 1* 24). As Bazin saw it, they favored techniques that forced reality to reveal its "structural depth." These techniques included the long take and deep focus, both of which located meaning objectively within the images themselves as opposed to imposing it through juxtaposition as in the case of montage. In other words, such techniques aimed to maintain, rather than manipulate, spatial-temporal relations. The long take, or sequence shot, preserved the continuity of dramatic action, thereby engendering "objectivity in time" (*What Is Cinema? v. 1* 14). Deep focus, on the other hand, kept multiple planes (e.g. foreground and background) simultaneously in focus, allowing for spatial unity within the image.

In Bazin's view, both devices marked an important "step forward in the history of film language" (*What Is Cinema? v. 1* 35). They not only made for a more realistic aesthetic practice, but also fundamentally altered how spectators related to these images. Bazin endorsed these attributes not because they simplified cinematic representation, but rather because they foregrounded the ambiguity and uncertainty that were a significant part of modern experience. In this regard, realism even shared some underlying traits with defamiliarization. "Only the impassive lens," writes Bazin, is capable of stripping away the preconceptions, "the spiritual dust and grime," which piles up and obscures the world around us (*What Is Cinema? v. 1* 15). It is only by seeing it anew that we might begin to reclaim our capacity to be part of the world and change it for the better.

Bazin's theoretical focus was further supported by the emergence of Italian neorealism, a style shared by a group of filmmakers that gained prominence in the immediate aftermath of World War II. The movement featured the work of directors Roberto Rossellini, Luchino Visconti, and Vittorio De Sica. Building on the traditions of poetic realism, these directors used non-professional actors and filmed on location to create a more direct or authentic account of reality. Another central figure in the movement, screenwriter Cesare Zavattini, further advocated for a turn away from overly contrived plots and the general artifice on which commercial cinema relied.[15] Bazin appreciated these specific practices, but he also suggested that there was something more to the neorealist approach. In De Sica's *Umberto D* (1955), for example, the film emphasizes "a succession of concrete instances of life," passing moments that lack obvious drama. But in presenting these "facts," the film transforms what can be considered as such. As the maid makes coffee, "The camera confines itself to watching her doing her little chores" (*What Is Cinema? v. 2* 81). These passing moments challenge our capacity to see the world as it really exists, and in certain instances, such as when the maid "shuts the door with the tip of her outstretched foot," the camera transforms these moments of life into "visible poetry" (*What Is Cinema? v. 2* 82).

Although Bazin was adamant in his defense of realist aesthetics, he was not necessarily doctrinaire in doing so. Categories like truth and reality were never absolute, but rather malleable and often contradictory. Bazin also understood that film was still evolving and that it was important to embrace new practices so long as they complemented the medium's main qualities. In an example of his willingness to adapt, he discusses the use of elision in Rossellini's *Paisà* (1946). While the technique is used to maintain "an intelligible succession of events," cause and effect "do not mesh like a chain with the sprockets of a wheel." Instead, the mind is forced "to leap from one event to the other as one leaps from stone to stone in crossing a river," knowing there is a chance that "one's foot hesitates between two rocks, or that one misses one's footing and slips" (*What Is Cinema? v. 2* 35–36). Bazin, contrary to his earlier emphasis on spatial and temporal unity, endorses the use of ellipsis as a way to heighten the viewer's role while also escaping the stringent cause-and-effect logic of **classical Hollywood cinema**. In his discussion of Rossellini, and in his later defense of Federico Fellini as a neorealist, Bazin foreshadows the use of ambiguity and indeterminacy that became a staple in post-war art cinema.

Bazin's ability to adapt was also an important practical skill as he became deeply involved in France's post-war film culture. Bazin had made it his mission to elevate the cultural status of film, organizing numerous cine-clubs and writing for a wide assortment of publications as part of a larger campaign to connect intellectuals with a

younger generation of aficionados. *Cahiers du cinéma*, the film journal that Bazin co-founded with Jacques Doniol-Valcroze and Lo
Duca in 1951, signaled a culmination of these efforts. It provided an
outlet for further developing the serious analysis of film and helped
to cultivate young critics Eric Rohmer, François Truffaut, Jean Luc
Godard, and Claude Charbol, a group that within the next decade
would comprise the leading directors of France's *nouvelle vague*, or
new wave style of filmmaking. Although Bazin had an immense
editorial influence at *Cahiers* and the journal generally subscribed
to his notion of realism, its younger contributors, the so-called
"young Turks," were also eager to make their own mark. It was
in part because of these efforts that the journal's defining concept
soon became *la politique des auteurs*. While the idea that certain
directors should be considered the principal creative author or that
some directors were decidedly more skilled than others was already
established, the *Cahiers* critics, despite Bazin's reservations, advanced
a much more audacious and antagonistic version of this view.

The *Cahiers* critics not only drew attention to successful Hollywood directors like Alfred Hitchcock, John Ford, and Howard
Hawks, but also made a point of elevating, at the time, less prominent directors like Samuel Fuller, Nicholas Ray, and Vincente
Minnelli. In this regard, these critics were becoming increasingly
self-conscious of their capacity to exert influence. This view of
authorship was contingent on their ability to identify a director's
unique style within the mise-en-scene and to discern thematic patterns across multiple films regardless of extraneous circumstances
such as the commercial imperatives of the Hollywood system. This
same principle extended to the delineation of new genres, most
notably film noir, as other categories worthy of critical investigation.
These categories were instrumental in expanding film criticism as a
critical endeavor and, by extension, in facilitating the development
of subsequent theoretical principles.

In this way, *Cahiers* had a profound impact on the serious study of
film. But its success was not without certain contradictions. By the
early 1960s the *Cahiers* notion of authorship had gained considerable
traction in Britain and the United States. In the hands of ***Andrew
Sarris***, the most prominent American proponent of authorship, the
concept took on a more doctrinaire, and occasionally chauvinistic,

tone. Authorship was used to erect a pantheon of great directors, in effect celebrating traditional aesthetic values in ways that were consistent with both the marketing interests of Hollywood and broader aesthetic conventions (i.e. that art was the province of individual genius). These more conservative undertones ran contrary to the increasingly radical politics that were taking hold throughout the 1960s in general and that were eventually embraced in journals like *Cahiers*. The emergence of these later perspectives eventually precipitated a more fundamental divide. Critics and theorists began to distinguish their work from what began to be labeled classical film theory. This term was partly a matter of periodization, designed to indicate the theoretical work that had taken place prior to 1960. But it also implicitly functioned as a pejorative. In effect, it was used to demarcate and reject ideas like authorship and realism that—at least from the vantage point of the late 1960s and 1970s—appeared naïve and incompatible with subsequent theoretical concerns. Although Bazin played a considerable role in instituting the framework that enabled these later interests, he was largely dismissed because of his perceived political inadequacies. As we have seen with a number of other early theorists, this was in many ways shortsighted and problematic. The work of correcting past misunderstandings is currently underway.[16]

SUMMARY

Over the course of the first half of the twentieth century a series of pioneering figures established film as a serious aesthetic and cultural practice. Although their interests and exact methods varied widely, early theorists succeeded in legitimizing a medium that had been considered disreputable because of its technological and commercial origins. They did this by identifying film's defining characteristics (i.e. its verisimilitude) and formal techniques (i.e. montage), and by developing a body of terms, concepts, and debates that served as the foundation for additional investigation. These were important steps in the later development of film study as an appropriate scholarly topic.

Questions

1. Why was it necessary to legitimize film? How did early theorists go about making their case and why were they ultimately successful?

2. Summarize the debate between the formalist and realist approach to film. What are the strengths and weaknesses of each side, and why was this debate possibly beneficial for film studies in the long run?

3. Why were filmmakers like Jean Epstein and Sergei Eisenstein so interested in theory? What was the relationship between their theoretical writings and their films?

4. What contextual factors contributed to the formation of film theory and the ability of early theorists to develop their ideas about film? Compare and contrast theorists working in two different national contexts (e.g. Germany and post-WWII France), and consider the different types of support that were available.

5. What were the formal devices and other specific qualities that early theorists found most interesting? Consider, for example, the close-up—how did different theorists describe it and what did they claim was its primary function?

NOTES

1 See Carroll (1988).
2 See Carroll (1996).
3 See Wasson (2005), Polan (2007), and Decherney (2005).
4 See Mitchell (1982) and May (1980).
5 See Abel (1988).
6 Breton, André. *Manifestos of Surrealism.* 21.
7 Aragon, Louis. "On Décor" in Hammond (2000).
8 See Epstein (2014), Keller and Paul (2012), and Wall-Romana (2013).
9 See David Bordwell's *Narration and the Fiction Film* (1985).
10 See Chapter 4 for further discussion of poetics and neoformalism.
11 Eisenstein, Sergei, Vsevolod Pudovkin, and Grigori Alexandrov. "Statement on Sound" in Eisenstein (1998).
12 See Winston (2001).

13 See Thomas Y. Levin's "Introduction" in Kracauer (1995), Miriam Hansen's "Introduction" in Kracauer (1997), and Hansen (2012).
14 See the discussion of Peter Wollen's *Signs and Meaning in the Cinema* in Chapter 3.
15 See Zavattini's "A Thesis on Neo-Realism" in Overbey (1979).
16 See, for example, Andrew (2011) and Morgan (2006).

FRENCH THEORY, 1949–68

For many, 1945 marked a decisive historical turning point. It was the end of World War II and, people hoped at least, the end of a tumultuous fifty-year period marred by violence, political strife, and economic instability. In this respect, the second half of the twentieth century promised the possibility of social and cultural renewal. Those like André Bazin seized this opportunity to revive France's post-war film culture and lay the groundwork for a new style of filmmaking. There were other signs like the increasing number of students attending university and growing economic affluence—in the United States especially—that suggested substantive progress was afoot. Some, however, took a very different view. From their perspective, the devastating effects of World War II had a more dire impact. Its association with systematic genocide and the introduction of atomic weapons suggested a fundamental failure and cast doubt on modern society's devotion to science as well as its premise of enlightened human reason. This more pessimistic viewpoint gained additional fodder as Cold War politics escalated, as the challenges of decolonization mounted, and as the general ruthlessness of capitalist enterprise continued unabated. For a significant number of French thinkers, these were the issues that took precedence in the post-war period.

French theory is an informal designation here. It does not indicate a systematized or formal body of thought, but instead refers to this group of thinkers and the intellectual developments they contributed to in the aftermath of World War II. The most important of these developments was the emergence of **structuralism**, a trans–disciplinary movement that took different orders of symbolic meaning as its primary object of study.[1] This approach largely began outside and along the margins of the French academy. Structuralism, as a result, remained a matter of ongoing debate throughout the period covered in this chapter and never really constituted a fully formed academic discipline. Even with this being the case, structuralism quickly became a pronounced influence among the leading exegetes of emerging fields like semiotics, psychoanalysis, and Marxism. As the Anglophone academy subsequently assimilated the tenets of these fields and structuralism more generally, it became clear that these developments represented more than just a new method of analysis. French theory also resonated because of its association with a series of broader social and institutional transitions. These reflected changes in how the university system and specific disciplines were organized as well as broader notions about how knowledge and scholarship should relate to art and politics.

French theory also represents a major shift in the overall direction of film theory. While the end of World War II is often used as a convenient dividing line that distinguishes classical and contemporary film theory, Chapter 1 has already suggested that early theory continues well into the 1950s. This simply means that there is a period of overlap whereby early theorists coexist with an unrelated set of theoretical developments. Although these different groups were not necessarily unaware of one another, they do represent very different traditions and institutional contexts. To fully understand the transition that takes place in the middle of the twentieth century, it is necessary, then, to step away from film and introduce the work of key figures like Claude Lévi-Strauss, Roland Barthes, Jacques Lacan, and Louis Althusser. In light of the material discussed in the chapter that follows, it should be clear that these thinkers played an integral role in shaping the major concepts and debates in the ensuing decades. Moreover, even though some sections entail a minor detour, the theoretical material covered here is never entirely divorced from film. These intersections became increasingly clear as French film critics and other commentators began to adopt terms and concepts directly from Lacan and Althusser. By the end of the 1960s, following the groundbreaking work of Christian Metz, these different strands had begun to merge more fully.

These developments were not only critical in advancing later theoretical interests; they also provided a basis for questioning and then rejecting many of the premises associated with earlier theorists. In this regard, French theory represents a more general shift away from the aesthetic merits of cinema. These earlier concerns were replaced with a growing interest in politics and film's affinity for the incendiary social protest movements that were prominent at this time. As a part of this larger cultural zeitgeist, both French theory as a whole and the emerging representatives of contemporary film theory placed great emphasis on the belief that aesthetics and politics were intertwined. Many of these intellectuals also believed that theoretical critique had an important role to play in the efforts to enact social change. As this period culminated with the events of May 1968, some of these beliefs began to wane. But for many film theorists, these ideals would continue to be axiomatic as they began to procure a place in the Anglophone academy.

THE LINGUISTIC TURN

Although structuralism is best known as one of the defining developments of post-war French theory, it also has a varied history that originates in the field of linguistics and the turn-of-the-century work of Swiss scholar *Ferdinand de Saussure*. This is why the rise of structuralism is often labeled the "linguistic turn," a designation that simultaneously indicates a fundamental break from earlier scholarly interests. In some ways, Saussure prefigured this break. His 1915 publication *Course in General Linguistics*, for instance, was an attempt to introduce a more scientific style of analysis to the study of language. In some respects, this foreshadowed the central role of the social sciences in shaping structuralism. For the most part, however, later French theorists adopted only select elements rather than his overall framework.

In his most widely recognized intervention, Saussure identified the basic linguistic unit as the **sign**, which in turn consisted of two parts: the **signifier**, meaning either a word as it is spoken or written as a combination of discrete phonemes, and the **signified**, the meaning or concept associated with that word. Saussure's second major intervention was to indicate that "the bond between the signifier and the signified is arbitrary" (*Course* 67). This means that there is no inherent or necessary connection between a series of individual letters, /t/r/e/e/ in Saussure's well-worn example, and the idea or concept associated with a given word, in this case a common plant featuring a trunk and lateral branches. As a result, listeners or readers may hold very different ideas of what a typical tree is or could be. And yet, that same audience is able to apprehend the basic significance of the word. The reason for this is twofold. First, meaning is established through various social conventions—traditional usages and other habitual practices that serve to reinforce a baseline consensus. Second, meaning is produced through context or, rather, through the position of words in relation to other words. In this regard, Saussure suggested that the value of a given term is "negative and differential," adding further that "in language there are only differences" (*Course* 119–20). This is true for both the signifier and the signified. At the level of the phoneme, the letter /f/ does not sound like /t/ and this allows us to distinguish different words such as "tree" and "free." Conceptually, meaning is likewise produced through opposition. "Mother," for instance, is defined less through its own intrinsic or positive value than by contrast to what it is not; for instance, its binary counterpart "father."

Saussure's terminology allowed for more rigorous forms of analysis, and it eventually became commonplace in efforts to expose the culturally constructed aspects of meaning. With particular regard to structuralism, however, Saussure made an even more important distinction between *langue*, translated either as language or language system, and *parole*, the French term for speech, the individual act of speaking sometimes referred to as enunciation. Saussure advocated a synchronic approach to linguistics in which the focus would be the fundamental principles that constitute the *langue* at a particular point in time. This shifted the emphasis away from a diachronic approach, which tended to track developments within speech across different time periods. For Saussure, the synchronic approach placed greater importance on language as a unified system of complex regulating structures. Although this overarching system is never entirely explicit or tangible, it provides a necessary pretense that structures the otherwise limitless possibilities inherent within speech. In chess, to use Saussure's analogy, the rules of the game establish which moves can be made. While some rules are abstract and static, the state of a game can change from move to move depending on the position of individual pieces. In effect, each move modifies when and how certain principles take precedence and the outcomes they can produce. It was this dialectic relationship between *langue* and *parole*—between the overarching system and its constituent parts— that informed Saussure's call for a broader study of signs, the science of semiology or, alternately, **semiotics**. Although he maintained that language comprised the most important system of signs, he also allowed that it should serve as a model for other branches of study similarly concerned with the laws that constitute and govern signs.

While Saussure provided the foundation for the linguistic turn, his influence was neither immediate nor direct. *Course in General Linguistics* was published posthumously, two years after Saussure had died, based on notes from several of his students (and it was not translated into English until 1959). As a result, Saussure's structural approach to language was without a guiding figure and his ideas, like some of the nascent concepts proposed by early film theorists, were left to slowly circulate in a somewhat stunted form. Saussure's modern approach to linguistics did, however, attract the interest of the Russian Formalists and Roman Jakobson in particular. Like Viktor Shklovsky, Jakobson was a key figure in the movement. Unlike Shklovsky, however, Jakobson gained international stature after leaving the Soviet Union in 1920. He went first to Czechoslovakia, where he helped to set up the Prague Linguistic Circle, one of Europe's main outposts for linguistic theory—the other was the Copenhagen school led by Louis Hjelmslev. By 1940, Jakobson, like many intellectuals, had immigrated to the United States to escape World War II. While teaching in New York, he met and became friends with **Claude Lévi-Strauss**. Jakobson introduced Lévi-Strauss to Saussure's structural approach just as the fledgling anthropologist was in the midst of writing his dissertation, *The Elementary Structures of Kinship*.[2]

Lévi-Strauss emerged as one of the dominant intellectual figures of the 1950s and 1960s and a leading proponent in establishing structuralism as the locus of post-war French theory. In applying the principles of structural linguistics to the field of anthropology, Lévi-Strauss was interested in the regulating structures that shape human relations. His first book, as the title indicates, focuses on the basic principles of kinship, which is to say the rules surrounding marriage rites or, more precisely, the rules that distinguish between proper and improper mating partners. For Lévi-Strauss, the most important structure in this regard was the incest taboo, the rule that prohibits members bound by consanguinity (i.e., a shared blood line or genetic lineage) from entering into marriage. As part of this overarching principle, society is divided into a series of opposing terms (e.g. brother, sister, father, son), each one constituting a structurally determined unit of kinship designed to reproduce the larger system (by marrying outside of their immediate family). The incest taboo further illustrates, then, the point at which culture imposes a regulatory structure that then determines and maintains what is considered natural.

Like Saussure, Lévi-Strauss placed greater emphasis on the overarching system that structures a particular state of variables. And, again like Saussure, Lévi-Strauss showed that the many variations of marriage rites served as evidence that there is an overriding rule that exists above and beyond any one situation. With these claims Lévi-Strauss was proposing a rather significant shift in the field of anthropology. He introduced a hybrid approach that combined elements of sociology, linguistics, and Freudian psychoanalysis. These theoretical influences served to partly displace the importance of fieldwork and empirical data. While his approach raised subsequent questions about the universal status of certain elementary structures, these concerns were overshadowed for a time by the ingenuity of this new method and its ability to challenge earlier assumptions within the field of anthropology. It was in this latter regard that structuralism was part of a broader transformation in which the adoption of new methods was also a means of questioning the orthodoxy of the existing educational system. Such challenges were not only evident in anthropology, but also in adjacent fields like history and psychology.

The challenge initiated by Lévi-Strauss thus precipitated additional shifts throughout the French academy and in the country's overall intellectual orientation. While philosophy had long served as the most venerable means of investigating abstract thought, structuralism provided an alternative avenue for pursuing new theoretical interests. This shift prompted a number of emerging scholars to turn away from traditions associated with the status quo. Structuralists, for instance, tended to disregard Henri Bergson, the most influential philosopher of the pre-war era, as well as prominent post-war philosophical movements like Jean-Paul Sartre's existentialism and Maurice Merleau-Ponty's phenomenology. In lieu of these influences, structuralists turned to German philosophy and the works of G. W. F. Hegel, Edmund Husserl, and Martin Heidegger. There were also institutional repercussions due to philosophy's entrenchment within the French academy. Because philosophy dominated the country's elite universities, structuralism tended to take root within the social sciences, which tended to be housed in less prestigious universities like the *École Pratique des Hautes Études* (School for Advanced Studies) where Lévi-Strauss was first appointed. These schools offered greater administrative and intellectual flexibility. They were also expanding during the post-war period. This made them all the more inviting to a new generation of scholars who had veered away from the traditional path to professional academic success and who were acutely interested in the new possibilities associated with structuralism.

Roland Barthes, who, like Lévi-Strauss, quickly rose to prominence in the 1950s and 1960s as a founding figure and key promoter of structuralism, was one of these scholars. Due to illness, Barthes had been unable to pursue a traditional university career. In 1948, he left Paris for interim teaching positions first in Romania and then Egypt. It was at the University of Alexandria where Barthes met the linguist A. J. Griemas and was first introduced to Saussure and Hjelmslev. After returning to France, Barthes began writing short, journalistic essays. These essays were collected, together with an explanatory essay, "Myth Today," and published in 1957 as *Mythologies*. Throughout these essays, Barthes draws attention to a diverse array of new consumer goods and other cultural ephemera to show just how France was changing in the post-war period. With this strategy, Barthes demonstrates the value of cultural analysis in generating an incisive reflection about the broader social order. In this regard, his efforts recall the overarching concerns of the Frankfurt School and, more specifically, the essayistic style used

by both Kracauer and Benjamin. This work also served as an important precursor to the Birmingham School and the rise of Cultural
Studies (discussed further in "Althusser and the Return to Marx"
of this chapter). What distinguished *Mythologies*, however, was the
specific way in which Barthes couched cultural analysis within a
structuralist framework.

In "Myth Today," Barthes suggests that culture and its various
subcategories are composed of signifying practices. Subcategories
like fashion and food, then, can be analyzed according to the same
structuralist principles that Lévi-Strauss used in his account of kinship. More specifically, this means that these subjects involve their
own regulating structures that determine and reinforce what its constituent components can signify. With regard to myth, Barthes is
interested in one particular example of how this process takes place.
In myth, signification purposefully disguises the structural underpin-
nings of its own operation. To put it another way, myth presents
meaning as a naturally occurring phenomenon when in fact it is
contrived as matter of culture, history, or politics. Barthes is also
interested in myth since it signals a shift away from Saussure and the
arbitrary relationship between signifier and signified. Myth always
entails a relationship based on motivation. This is also the case with
images. For both, this means that the relationship between a representation and its referent is shaped by supplemental factors. With
most images, for example, the relationship between representation
and referent is based on the principle of visual resemblance. To this
end, Barthes introduced a model based on Hjelmslev's connotative
semiotics in which myth is associated with a second order of meaning, a system of communication affixed to Saussure's linguistic model
but that involves an additional layer of signification. According to
this model, the sign is not just a culmination of signifier and signified, but simultaneously an intermediary in the exchange between
denotation and **connotation**. The sign denotes one meaning in a
way that accommodates a number of implicit, associated meanings
or connotations. This process happens in a way, however, that masks
the degree to which this is the work of signification.

Barthes poses several image-based examples to illustrate this process. In "Myth Today," he discusses a 1955 cover of the French
magazine, *Paris Match*. On its surface, the image denotes a young

black soldier standing in salute, ostensibly in honor of a French flag raised somewhere beyond the frame of the photograph. As Barthes observes, the image also functions in a highly ideological manner. At the time, France was engaged in complex questions about its imperialist legacy. It had recently relinquished its territorial claims in Vietnam and was in the midst of an aggressive campaign to suppress the independence movement in Algeria. The cover image, according to Barthes, signifies "that France is a great Empire" by virtue of the fact that all of its citizens, regardless of race, serve it faithfully and without question (*Mythologies* 116). In this respect, the image asks its viewer to accept this as if "it goes without saying"—as if French imperialism is an indisputable matter of fact. This implicates the viewer as the means by which the image's secondary meaning solidifies into myth.

In his 1964 essay, "Rhetoric of the Image," Barthes again analyzes an individual image, this time a print advertisement for the French brand of pasta, Panzani. In this case, he further adapts his earlier linguistic model and identifies three different messages within the advertisement: the linguistic message (the text or captions that appear), the denoted or non-coded iconic message (the photographic image itself), and the coded or symbolic iconic message (the connotations inscribed as part of the exchange between different messages). As with the *Paris Match* cover, Barthes is particularly attentive to how these different levels of meaning work together to produce an abstract quality that he terms "Italianicity," the stereotypical essence of a foreign culture that is used as part of the advertisement's rhetoric. Here Barthes also notes the role of photography in naturalizing the symbolic messages. He discusses the photographic image in terms that foreground its indexicality yet also emphasizes how this technology is used primarily to mask "the constructed meaning under the appearance of the given meaning" (*Image/Music/Text* 46). In other words, photography functions primarily in the service of myth, as part of the same ideological mechanism that "transforms petit-bourgeois culture into a universal nature" (*Mythologies* 9).

Both Lévi-Strauss and Barthes were instrumental in the rise of structuralism. Lévi-Strauss imported Saussure's linguistic model and made it a foundation for post-war French theory. Barthes, a beneficiary of the shifting priorities taking place within France's intellectual scene, made it clear that culture was neither the exclusive domain of academic orthodoxy nor only the subject of distant fieldwork. He drew attention to how culture in its most recent incarnations was becoming increasingly pervasive. Moreover, he demonstrated how it participated in complex semiotic formations that could tell us something about the overarching ideological system of values, beliefs, and ideas that helped to maintain the existing status quo. By adapting and further developing the linguistic model introduced by Saussure and Lévi-Strauss, Barthes demonstrated more fully the value of this structural approach. Together, they provided a technical vocabulary and an analytical framework that allowed for more rigorous forms of cultural inquiry.

Though Barthes' attention to mass culture and images in particular made his analyses more directly relevant to film scholars, it wasn't until the later work of Metz that structuralism would come to have its full theoretical impact. This delay was compounded by two other complications in the reception of Barthes and structuralism more generally. First, as a theoretical rubric, structuralism was never entirely stable. Despite its appeals to methodological rigor, structuralism was perpetually changing, often at a rate that outpaced its English translators. Barthes, for instance, gradually moved away from structuralism entirely. His later works are instead classified as **post-structuralism**, a distinction that Barthes and many others from his generation embraced as they made the limits and ambiguities already implicit within structuralism the focal point of their work. Second, while Barthes provided further legitimization for the study of popular culture, his account illustrated a stark difference between his theoretically informed approach and contemporaneous developments taking place among film critics. For Barthes, cultural texts are valuable to the extent that they illustrate the ideological operations implicit in various forms of signification. As noted in the previous chapter, French film critics and their Anglo-American adherents were by contrast still predominantly focused on *la politique des auteurs*, the belief that film's significance resided in the skill and artistry of its director. Barthes further underscored the irrevocable differences between the two approaches with his later essay provocatively titled "Death of the Author."[3]

LACAN AND THE RETURN TO FREUD

Cinema has always had an affinity for dreams, distortions, and delusion. And, as a result, it has a long history of intersection with psychoanalysis.[4] As mentioned in the previous chapter, Sigmund Freud and psychoanalytic theory quickly drew the interest of Frankfurt School intellectuals like Walter Benjamin and elicited more passing references by Eisenstein and Bazin. The British critic H. D. began a more sustained consideration of psychoanalysis in the journal *Close-Up* in the 1920s and 1930s.[5] Surrealist artists such as Luis Buñuel and Salvador Dalí in their collaboration *Un Chien andalou* meanwhile embraced psychoanalysis as a source of creative inspiration. Psychoanalysis even attracted the interest of Hollywood executives. Samuel Goldwyn, for example, approached Freud in 1925 with an offer to serve as a consultant on one of its productions. For the most part, however, these early intersections remained mostly cursory. It was only after World War II and the work of French psychoanalyst ***Jacques Lacan*** that this specialized discourse evolved into a much more prominent theoretical force. Although he characterized his efforts as part of a return to Freud and the fundamental principles of psychoanalysis, a major part of Lacan's appeal was his ability to put psychoanalysis in dialogue with the latest developments in structuralism. These mixed messages were typical of Lacan's recalcitrant, sometimes insufferable, personal style.

For Freud, psychoanalysis was primarily a therapeutic technique. It was one that drew on Freud's experience as a trained medical doctor and scientific researcher, as well as his wide-ranging interest in neurology and psychiatry. It was an invention that also marked a revolutionary departure from existing dogma regarding human behavior and the nature of mental life. In one of Freud's most important breakthroughs, he posited that the human psyche is divided between conscious and unconscious domains. This divide makes for a dynamic negotiation between conflicting interests: for example, between an individual's libido or drive for immediate pleasure and the relentless pressure to conform to social norms. Freud subsequently revised his map of the human mind into three parts—the id, ego, and superego (whereas the first two parts roughly correspond with his earlier division, the last element emphasizes the way individuals internalize social and cultural mores). Even with this new topography, his main insight still held: the unconscious was a repository for the thoughts, desires, and fantasies that were deemed unacceptable by the conscious mind and by society at large. As part of the effort to stave off these materials, the psyche developed a number of defense mechanisms (e.g. inhibition, sublimation, obsessive-compulsive fixation), all of which were related to the broader process referred to as **repression**. For Freud, it was the failure or malfunctioning of these processes that was typically at the root of neurosis and other mental afflictions.

Psychoanalytic treatment consisted of regular sessions in which the patient—or in later French parlance, the *analysand*—is encouraged to speak freely about anything that comes to mind. During these sessions the analyst listens quietly to discern **symptomatic** revelations, or the surfacing of unconscious materials. The methods Freud developed to analyze these materials, and the various resistances and distortions that accompanied them, were first presented as part of his virtuoso work, *The Interpretation of Dreams*. For Freud, dreams are an exercise in wish fulfillment, often expressing desires that are unconscious or repressed. But they also tend to appear in a disguised form, one that required Freud to distinguish between a dream's manifest content (i.e., the parts the patient is able to recount during analysis) and its latent content. To fully understand the work that takes place as part of the dream, Freud identified **displacement** and **condensation** as two types of necessary encryption, mechanisms that both acknowledged and concealed the dream's latent content. The reason for such elaborate maneuvering was because the most unconscious desires were of a sexual nature and, therefore, taboo. In another of Freud's major contributions, he maintained that human beings were from the earliest stages of infancy exceptionally sexual creatures. This was decidedly scandalous for both turn-of-the-century Vienna and bourgeois sensibilities more generally, but it also identified what was at the root of most individual and social dysfunction. The need to constantly censor this material only compounded these problems.

Even while introducing the prevalence of infantile sexuality, Freud was attuned to how a child's uninhibited urges are eventually aligned with prevailing social conventions. He argued that children pass through a succession of stages in which a different erogenous zone takes precedence—the first being oral, the second anal, and the final one being genital. This last stage involved Freud's most famous theory, the **Oedipal complex**. Inspired by Sophocles' Greek tragedy, *Oedipus Rex*, this formulation stipulates that the male child attaches a sexual desire to his mother. The child, however, must learn to redirect that desire to a socially acceptable recipient, one who does not jeopardize the incest taboo or any other moral standards. This process is typically triggered by the father who threatens the child with **castration**, a threat that is more often symbolic than real but that no less promises to vacate the child's most direct claim to paternal accession, his genitalia.

Freud developed much of his thinking through clinical observations that in turn became the basis for several key case studies (e.g. "The Rat Man" and "The Wolf Man"). Despite the ostensibly empirical basis of these observations, many of his theories, like the Oedipal complex, were largely speculative and presented as universal even when evidence was imprecise or problematic. As Freud continued to modify and expand his theories throughout his later career, he expanded psychoanalysis beyond its clinical applications, engendering further speculation often by engaging art, culture, and religion. For example, in his investigation of Leonardo da Vinci, Freud details a biographical note contained in the artist's scientific notebooks, an early memory of a strange encounter with a vulture in which the bird physically assaults Leonardo as a baby still in his cradle. Freud posits that the anecdote is in fact a screen memory, a fantasy that is retroactively cast as memory. And in the course of an elaborate reconstruction of this fantasy, Freud contends that the bird contains a double meaning which link the erotic undertones of the fantasy to both homosexuality and Leonardo's mother. In both respects, it is clear to Freud that childhood events had a decisive impact on Leonardo's later life as well as his professional predilections including his knack for conjuring beguiling smiles upon the lips of his female subjects, most famously in his portrait of Mona Lisa. This interpretation provides a brief illustration of Freud's explanatory power and how his methods of analysis could be applied to art and literature.

Although Freud enjoyed some degree of success in establishing the merits of psychoanalysis, there were also numerous challenges.

For many, it was unclear whether Freud was exposing the hypocrisy of Western civilization or providing it with a therapeutic means of reinforcing its existing rules. Freud made a concerted effort throughout his career to address these questions and respond to his various critics. He frequently accepted invitations to lecture on behalf of psychoanalysis and produced accessible versions of his more technical tracts. He also helped to establish a network of regional and international psychoanalytic societies. Their purpose was to codify standard practices and techniques, preserve the field's autonomy and, thus, the appearance of respectability among supporters and its clientele. This instilled a certain amount of professional integrity, but often came at the expense of curtailing Freud's more daring implications.

These organizations would also play a significant role for Jacques Lacan both as he entered the professional field in the 1930s and later in his life as he repeatedly challenged their authority. This contentious relationship was not only an extension of Lacan's predilection for antagonism but also part of the complicated reception of psychoanalysis in France. Whereas avant-garde dissidents like the Surrealists welcomed Freudian psychoanalysis, France's medical and academic establishments had been far more apprehensive. France had its own traditions pertaining to psychological study and the country remained generally hostile to all German thought. As a result, most of Freud's writing, especially during the first half of the twentieth century, was simply not available in French. Similar to the structuralists' turn away from philosophy in favor of the social sciences, Lacan's turn to Freudian psychoanalysis was part of a rejection of France's insular orthodoxy.

By extension, Lacan adopted a decidedly more inter-disciplinary approach to psychoanalytic theory. He conferred with Salvador Dalí while writing his dissertation on paranoia and made frequent reference to surrealism throughout his career. Lacan referred to German philosophy even more extensively; for example, drawing upon Alexandre Kojève's account of the master–slave dialectic in Hegel as the basis for his understanding of inter-subjective relations.[6] These influences indicate that even while advocating a return to Freud, Lacan was poised to develop his own distinctive brand of psychoanalysis. It was one that would seek to recover Freud's quintessential insights without endorsing his views as immutable doctrine. It would simultaneously reject the principles being prescribed by the discipline's governing bodies. This was fully apparent, for instance, in Lacan's dismissal of ego psychology, a psychoanalytic offshoot that gained ground in America after World War II. Lacan's version of psychoanalysis would, moreover, embrace the latest intellectual innovations and remain closely aligned with the broader aims of French theory.

Although Lacan had presented an earlier version of the same paper in 1936, much of his intellectual reputation began with the 1949 presentation of "The Mirror Stage as Formative of the Function of the I" at the International Psychoanalytical Association's sixteenth congress. The **mirror stage** certainly represents one of Lacan's most important contributions and the main gateway by which film theorists came to appreciate his significance. In general, it refers to a particular point within a child's early development (i.e., between the age of six and eighteen months) that explains the formation of the ego. As Lacan further details it, the child encounters its image in the mirror and recognizes itself as an independent and unified whole despite the fact that he or she lacks the physical coordination to function autonomously. Although there are some references to empirical data in the essay, the mirror stage more generally suggests a hypothetical event that illustrates a basic incongruity in how subjectivity is structured. Many have taken this general condemnation of subjectivity to be a larger attack on the belief that selfhood is an intrinsic or self-determined development. In this regard, Lacan was part of the turn to **anti-humanism**, a general tendency among French theorists to question or reject the underlying principles of Western thought. To further reiterate this point, Lacan claims that the subject is plagued by misrecongition. The image that the child encounters in the mirror is not the self, but in fact an **other**. This means that the image in the mirror instills both a narcissistic infatuation for an impossible ideal and an inescapable sense of deficiency or alienation. Lacan more broadly characterized this exchange as part of an Imaginary state, one that preceded the child's entry into a Symbolic realm defined by language. These two orders coexisted with and yet were irreducible to a third order, the Real. These distinctions gained additional significance in Lacan's subsequent thought, forming the basis for his psychoanalytic theory in the same way that Freud's three-part topography (i.e., of the id, ego, and superego) formed for him the basis of the human psyche.

Throughout the 1950s Lacan continued to place a growing emphasis on language. This was related to his interest in returning to Freud's original words and to the importance of verbalization within the *analysand*'s account, but was also the result of his introduction to linguistics and Saussure more specifically by way of his friendship with Claude Lévi-Strauss and Roman Jakobson. Of course, as he began to engage this new material, Lacan was not content to simply apply linguistics according to accepted conventions. In one of his better-known interventions, for example, Lacan reversed Saussure's formulation of the sign so that the signified or meaning no longer precedes the signifier, the formal unit or intermediary necessary for signification. In some respects, the mirror stage already anticipates this reversal. It essentially places one's image ahead of oneself. And as one's image continues to accrue cultural currency or exchange value, it takes precedence over the thing to which it refers. By this same logic, the subject is cast as a signifier, an intermediary barred from full meaning or being. It merely exists for other signifiers within a network of signification or signifying chain. This particular account is simultaneously indebted to Jakobson's work on shifters, grammatical units such as personal pronouns that denote the speaking subject but only by reference to the context within which these units are enunciated.

Just as Jakobson provided part of the foundation for Lacan's linguistic-based theory of the subject, his account of metaphor and metonymy provided a catalyst for expanding the basic operations that Freud had identified in his dream-work. As a corollary to displacement and condensation, these figures emphasize two distinct orders within language. The logic of both the metaphor and displacement is defined as paradigmatic. They entail substitution based on similarity. The logic of metonymy and condensation, by contrast, is syntagmatic. They are based on sequential contiguity. In this respect, these linguistic figures are no longer resigned to the interpretation of dreams, but point to the importance of discursive structures in shaping all of human experience.

As part of Lacan's expanding engagement with the role of language, many of his ideas became even more complex. For example, he associates language, on the one hand, with the unconscious. It is, he says, structured like a language. Or, rather, in the same sense that *langue* or language as a whole exceeds any one speaker, "the unconscious is the discourse of the Other," a field like language that determines that speaker without ever being fully present (*Language of the Self* 27). On the other hand, Lacan also associates language with the law or the "name of the father." Both of these figures are representative of the way the symbolic order holds the power to constrain or dictate meaning according to existing cultural hierarchies. This power is also evident in the case of the **phallus**. Though Lacan attempted to distinguish this figure from its anatomical analog, the penis, it remains closely tied to standard notions of sexual difference. As a signifier, access to the phallus follows a path similar to the mirror stage. It entails a transaction whereby some semblance of plenitude is acquired in exchange for perpetual dissatisfaction in the form of unrequited desire. Insofar as it functions as the paternal signifier, however, the male sex is endowed with a symbolic currency that covers over the negative effects implicit in this tradeoff. The female sex, by contrast, is defined exclusively in terms of lack. As a result, even while Lacan provides a framework for discerning the constructed nature of male privilege, the phallus still continues to support a system of **patriarchy**.

While the visual emphasis of the mirror stage and the incorporation of linguistic terminology primed psychoanalysis for its eventual uptake by film theorists, Lacan, like Freud, did not directly concern himself with cinema or its implications. With that being said, there were also elements in Lacan's work that were more open to adoption than anything provided by his predecessor. For instance, with regard to the relationship between language and the law, Lacan used the term *point de capiton*, translated as the quilting or buttoning point, to describe the point at which meaning is pinned down, anchored or punctuated, as it were.[7] In a commentary on Lacan's 1964 seminar, Jacques-Alain Miller introduced the term **suture** to name "the relation of the subject to the chain of its discourse" where "it figures there as the element which is lacking, in the form of a stand-in" ("Suture" 25–6). Although Miller introduces mathematical figures to further elaborate this formulation, the term also hearkens back to the logic of the quilting point. It explains a system in which a signifier is assigned meaning, but only as a proxy for what is necessarily absent and excluded within that system.

In a 1969 *Cahiers du cinéma* article, Jean-Pierre Oudart then transported the concept to film. The comparison is based on the premise that cinematic discourse operates like linguistic discourse: it is the formal configuration of images that constitute the subject-position and meaning is produced as a condition of the viewer's absence. To put it another way, the viewer is inserted, or stitched to be precise, into cinematic discourse by virtue of their exclusion from the production of meaning. The particular case of suture illustrates both the relevance of certain Lacanian concepts for film and the alacrity with which these linkages were taken up. In the period that will be addressed in the following chapter, film theorists such as Daniel Dayan, Stephen Heath, Kaja Silverman, and, later, Slavoj Žižek significantly added to the initial account provided by Oudart.[8] These later elaborations also benefitted from subsequent theoretical developments, for example the recognition that cinematic discourse and the system of suture correspond to the ideological operations that will be discussed in the following section.

Throughout the 1960s Lacan developed an immense following that easily made him as influential as Claude Lévi-Strauss and Roland Barthes. In fact, the 1966 publication of Lacan's *Ecrits*, the first volume to systematically make his earlier essays and articles available, became a bestseller in France. Unlike Lévi-Strauss and Barthes, however, Lacan operated entirely outside of the university system. This provided him with a greater degree of intellectual autonomy and the freedom to develop an unusually idiosyncratic cult of personality. It also meant that Lacan maintained a different relationship between theory and practice. As a practicing clinician, Lacan was beholden to his patients and to a different set of bureaucratic standards. As mentioned earlier, these obligations became a major source of controversy throughout Lacan's career. Lacan persistently challenged the standard session length and various other training protocols as prescribed by the field's governing bodies. This led to several contentious splits including his 1963 "excommunication" from the International Psychoanalytic Association. Lacan's struggle with authority may have bolstered his anti-establishment reputation and enhanced his standing with a growing contingent of radicalized students. These factors certainly played some role in his appeal to subsequent film theorists.

ALTHUSSER AND THE RETURN TO MARX

The theoretical innovations associated with semiotics and psychoanalysis in the 1950s and 1960s provided a foundation for challenging dominant social structures. They provided both a critical terminology and a series of analytical techniques that were considered more rigorous and relevant than existing methodologies. More importantly, these practices dovetailed with the growing discord among students and dissidents who were beginning to question the status quo in an increasingly confrontational manner. This penchant for opposition was further exacerbated as both sides in the festering Cold War engendered disillusionment and discontent. For instance, while the West operated under the auspices of democratic principles, it was engaged in many unscrupulous policies and tended to put the interests of capitalism ahead of its own citizens. Soviet Russia was equally problematic. Many of its policies had become tryannical, and it had become increasingly repressive in controlling the Eastern bloc. These developments prompted many to turn away from partisan politics per se and to begin asking more fundamental questions about the nature of power. And in seeking new forms of liberation, there was a willingness at this time to consider more radical alternatives. This line of questioning was by no means exclusive to France, but once again it was a French theorist, **Louis Althusser**, who came to personify many of these concerns and who would have the most galvanizing impact on contemporary film theory.

By the mid-1960s, Althusser had developed an influential position among students. Like several of his peers, however, Althusser had struggled as something of an outlier in the years prior to his acclaim. The war and ongoing health issues had negatively affected Althusser's early professional career. As a result, he spent most of his life in the marginal role of philosophy *caïman*, a kind of tutor assisting students in their preparation for qualifying exams, at the *École normale supérieure*. Althusser was also unusual because of his commitment to the French Communist Party (or PCF for *Parti communiste français*). The relationship between intellectuals and socialist politics had become increasingly strained following revelations of impropriety on the part of the Soviet Union, and as the PCF became preoccupied with its own internal power struggles. Consequently, Althusser was somewhat isolated from other scholars and constrained by the Party's priorities. Even with these obstacles, however, Althusser began to facilitate an important transition. He introduced his students to Marx and Lenin, renewing interest among a nascent generation of scholars while also demonstrating the relevance of Marxist thought for current political struggles. In doing so, he helped the PCF to rekindle a tenuous alliance with intellectuals, for example by modifying the editorial policy of its journal *La Nouvelle Critique* and by forging an intermittent partnership with *Tel Quel*, the leading intellectual journal of the period.[9]

While Althusser began this period as a somewhat marginal and politically embattled figure, he soon gained prominence by developing an affinity for the new structuralist paradigm. In this regard, he advocated a return to Marx, which, like Lacan's return to Freud, was couched in the terms and methods of post-war French theory. First, Althusser identified an epistemological break that distinguished two separate periods in Marx's thinking. According to this view, Marx's early writings were shaped by philosophy's existing conventions and therefore tainted. By 1845, however, Marx turned his attention to founding a new philosophy, dialectical materialism, or what Althusser terms the science of history. This distinction helped Althusser to sidestep some of the stigma left by later Soviet leaders while also dislodging Marx from a tradition of liberal humanism. In terms of re-framing Marxist thought as a scientific endeavor, Althusser had two additional aims. First, it was a revision that allowed him to complicate more mechanistic Marxist accounts in which all social relations were exclusively determined by economic conditions. Second, it served to acclimate Marxist discourse to the social scientific underpinnings of structuralism—appealing to its reputation for more strenuous forms of analysis as well as its anti-establishment associations. Science in this respect was not a matter of recasting Marxism as a rationalist system. Instead, it was a matter of characterizing its principles as theory, meaning the concepts for which revolutionary struggle was the necessary practice.

As an extension of these two aims, Althusser introduced the notion of structural causality. This concept explains how the mode of production, or capitalist system, determines the form and relational logic of its products while often remaining imperceptible. This is variously referred to as an absent cause or the structuring absence. This formulation overlaps with Lacan's account of the subject as an effect of a signifying chain, which was consistent with several efforts by Althusser to link Marx with psychoanalytic concepts like over-determination. The phrase structuring absence was subsequently applied in a broad range of contexts and it became particularly useful for later film theorists like Laura Mulvey, for instance, in her elaboration of the male gaze (see "Feminist film theory" in Chapter 3).

In terms of revitalizing Marxist theory, the most important concept for Althusser is **ideology**. One of the general questions, especially in the West, at this time concerned the persistence of economic disparity despite democratic principles. From a Marxist perspective, the ruling class maintains its position by subordinating another group—the working class or proletariat—such that they lack access to the means of fundamentally changing the system. In certain cases, like slavery, the subordinate group is dominated through physical violence, coercion, and legal disenfranchisement. Democratic governments, however, promise citizens the right to participate equally in determining the rule of law. In principle, any group subject to injustice will use this right to change the system. For Althusser, ideology is a major factor in why history does not progress according to this logic. It also explains why the ruling class is able to maintain its power and perpetuate a system of social stratification regardless of the government's legislative policies. To explain this further he draws a distinction between conventional forms of state power, for instance military forces and the police, and ideological instruments or what he broadly refers to with the catchall **Ideological State Apparatus** (ISA).

Whereas the military and police use repressive force, ideology facilitates a different way of soliciting compliance. ISAs consist of institutions such as the nuclear family, religion, the educational system, and the media. These institutions reinforce "the rules of the established order," not in a punitive sense but by establishing the social ideals and norms that supposedly supersede class or material conditions (*Lenin and Philosophy* 89). In subscribing to these ideals, Althusser contends that we accept an imaginary relationship to the real conditions of existence (*Lenin and Philosophy* 109). In this regard, family, religion, and all of the other ISAs were more than a matter of false consciousness, as Marx had deemed ideology. Instead, these institutions are structurally necessary in perpetuating a larger system of exploitation and oppression. In effect, they provide a social situation or context in which it appears material conditions are irrelevant or non-existent. These situations are labeled imaginary, not in the sense that they are unreal or fanciful, but because they disguise the fact that they too are a byproduct of political and economic conditions. And it is not just that ISAs disguise these real conditions but that these conditions continue to operate precisely because they are able to avoid direct scrutiny. As a critical concept then, ideology, somewhat similar to Freud's dream analysis, provided tremendous explanatory power. In general, it helped to explain the persistence of fundamental inequalities. It is also important in the sense that it illustrates why certain groups are compelled to support the status quo often at the expense of their own interests.

Althusser further developed his account by arguing that ideology was also manifest in more concrete forms. For instance, each of the institutions described as an ISA involves a series of practices or rituals that furnished its ideas with a material dimension. Althusser described this process as **interpellation** or, rather, the way in which individuals are constituted as subjects. The term "subject" has many meanings, but in this instance it evokes the way in which a person is conferred legal status as the object or property of a sovereign power (i.e., all the king's subjects). To illustrate, he provides a prototypical example in which a police officer calls out, "Hey, you there!" This statement serves to hail or recruit an innocent bystander to answer as the "you," to turn around and thus become the subject of the interrogative phrase. This example suggests that individuals, by recognizing themselves as the subject within this exchange, are always also, in a formulation that explicitly recalls Lacan's mirror stage, the product of a misrecognition. The broader implication is again that ideology grants individuals some modicum of social status but only by inserting them into an existing system of relations in which they are both subservient to and complicit in maintaining the status quo.

This formulation also became important for later accounts of suture. The film theorists that adopted this term drew attention to how cinematic discourse, like ideology, provides the audience members with a degree of agency, for example the ability to see multiple perspectives. But it does this in a way whereby the viewer ultimately remains subject to the apparatus, in this case the camera and its controlling logic.

These parallels with suture are also emblematic of ideology's broader resonance during this period. To reiterate, ideology illustrates the ways in which power renders its own operations transparent and how it is this feature that allows certain systems of domination to persist. In this regard, ideology closely paralleled the naturalizing function that Barthes identified within certain forms of signification (e.g. myth). There were also similarities with the ideas of *Antonio Gramsci*, an Italian Marxist who wrote while imprisoned during the 1930s but whose work really only began to circulate posthumously after World War II. Gramsci is primarily associated with **hegemony**, a concept, like ideology, that explains how social control is often cultivated through mutual consent rather than direct force. It works for instance when a powerful group, like the wealthiest individuals or ruling class, persuades other groups to accept their values as mere common sense. This means that one group is able to convince all of society to accept their ideas as inherent or self-evident and beyond questioning. Though hegemony provides another instance in which a subordinate group or class participates in its own subjugation, Gramsci also placed greater emphasis on the possibility of counter-hegemony—ideas capable of challenging or subverting the dominant ideology.

As has already been mentioned, Althusser also used ideology to elaborate an explicit correlation with psychoanalysis, in effect translating Lacan's formulation of the subject into a more overtly political register. Following this logic, certain subsequent accounts took ideology to be tantamount to language, with both serving as instruments of domination whereby individuals were reduced to mere pawns devoid of agency or self-determination. Another major French theorist, *Michel Foucault*, provided additional support for these corollaries, albeit from a perspective that was driven by historical analysis rather than Lacanian psychoanalysis. He examined, for instance, how sexuality and mental health were constructed as part of discourse and drew particular attention to the institutional terminology and techniques that served to inscribe the differences between normal and abnormal upon the body. In his most famous account, *Discipline and Punish*, Foucault explores these dynamics in relation to power. More specifically, he details the transition that took place between the "spectacle of the scaffold," the pre-modern era in which executions and other forms of punishment were carried out in public, and the modern disciplinary regime that he associates with the **panopticon**, a hypothetical penal system in which individual cells are arranged around a central tower so that all prisoners are subject to observation at any time. In an even more concrete sense than Althusser's notion of interpellation, Foucault illustrates the material and institutional basis of structural domination. In this case it exists as part of the architecture of the prison. This structure, or what is variously referred to as an apparatus or *dispositif* (the French term for device), in turn establishes a system of relationships that extend beyond its material dimensions. In this particular instance, inmates internalize a state of perpetual surveillance that renders them more fundamentally docile and obedient than the previous system of overt punishment.

Although there were important variations among these different theorists, terms like "power" and "ideology" came to acquire a more general currency by the late 1960s. This was certainly evident as film theorists began to embrace **apparatus theory** as a general basis for attacking the ideological dimensions of cinema and its dominant styles. In a series of influential essays written in the aftermath of May 1968, *Jean-Louis Baudry* identifies two parallels that would become axiomatic for subsequent theoretical analysis. First, he likens the cinematic camera to an optical apparatus shaped by traditions dating back to the early Renaissance. The camera, in this respect, produces an impression of reality rooted in the **Quattrocento** style, a technique that uses linear perspective to create the illusion of depth and that gave rise to a heightened sense of realism in Western painting. This is also to say that the images produced by the camera are neither entirely neutral nor a direct reflection of objective reality. Instead, and in diametric opposition to earlier theorists like Bazin, this means that the image is a construction or product made to the order of precise ideological specifications. This assessment further coincided with Guy Debord's sweeping condemnation of what he termed the "society of the spectacle," or the way in which modern life had become a wholesale falsification subsumed by the logic of capital.[10]

The second parallel, according to Baudry, stems from the fact that the cinematic apparatus is more than just the camera and what it records. The cinematic apparatus instead encompasses the entire production process as well as the way in which individual viewers are situated in relation to its image. With respect to the latter relationship, Baudry emphasizes that even while cinematic images are presented as unified and whole, they are largely the result of an illusory process. Film as a medium consists of a series of individual photographs which, when projected together at a certain speed, produce the appearance of continuous motion. Narrative film is even more egregious in that it elides the intense editing and post-production procedures necessary to produce a cohesive story world. In this regard, the viewer is not only denied access to the means of production but these means are entirely suppressed by the false impression of spatial and temporal continuity. For Baudry, this recalls Althusser's formulation of ideology, fostering an imaginary relationship with the images on screen while effacing the real conditions of their production. At the same time, he posited a general analogy with Lacan's account of the mirror stage. According to this comparison, the viewer is captivated by the ideal images that appear on screen such that their own limitations are concealed. This means that the viewer is largely powerless to do anything other than briefly identify with an ideologically determined surrogate. In highlighting these parallels, Baudry drew attention to the cinematographic apparatus as another key instance of structural domination. It was another tool that served to maintain an existing state of affairs while also masking its own methods of operation.

While Althusser had a decisive impact on subsequent film scholarship, his account of ideology was also part of a more diffuse return to Marxist analysis of culture and society. British **cultural studies**, for example, arose at approximately the same time as French theory and was similarly invested in revising Marx's orthodox economic principles to renew his relevance for contemporary scholarly interests. While the two developments shared many of the same basic goals, they also illustrate some significant variations as different schools of thought laid claim to the same theoretical terrain. In terms of similarities, cultural studies like structuralism emerged as an informal distinction that was attached to a group of scholars (e.g. Richard Hoggart, Raymond Williams, and E. P. Thompson) and the work they began publishing at the end of the 1950s. Like some of their French counterparts, these scholars had followed an unlikely professional trajectory, coming from working-class backgrounds and spending their early academic careers teaching in less prestigious adult education programs. Many of their earliest works addressed culture in its everyday, ordinary sense much in the same way as Roland Barthes had in *Mythologies*. Unlike Barthes, however, there was no appeal to the scientific undertones of structuralism. The British scholars were instead rooted in more traditional models of literary and historical study, and their main concern was to reclaim culture for the working class. In this respect, class-consciousness had a very different valence. It came to signify a positive attribute in the formation of identity rather than a means of revolutionary social change. By extension, cultural studies tended to emphasize the liberating possibilities of counter-hegemony and other forms of resistance rather than the repressive structures that maintained the status quo.[11]

In 1964, Richard Hoggart founded the Centre for Contemporary Cultural Studies at the University of Birmingham. The Centre served to solidify the movement into a more formally recognized academic model and provided a degree of institutional stability as cultural studies expanded significantly over the next two decades. At the same time, theory as a general field was also expanding. This sometimes created a bewildering array of shifting alliances and divisions. The establishment of the Birmingham Centre, for instance, marked a break with the *New Left Review*, which under the editorship of Perry Anderson had begun a more overt embrace of French theory and its politicized overtones. This divide was exacerbated in later works like *The Poverty of Theory*, where E. P. Thompson rejected Althusser's theoretical position as abstract, a-historical, and overly pessimistic. By contrast, when **Stuart Hall** replaced Hoggart as director of the Centre in 1969, cultural studies began to incorporate Barthes and Althusser. In doing so, it also began to shift away from class to address more specific issues related to race, ethnicity, gender, sexuality, and the mass media.[12] Even though French theory would have a more direct effect on film theory, the emergence of adjacent fields like cultural studies illustrates the broadening influence of theory as a whole in the post-war period. Moreover, as these various influences moved into different national and disciplinary contexts, they were often mixed together or even taken to be interchangeable.

CINEMA AND SEMIOTICS

Amidst this broader flurry of intellectual activity, **Christian Metz** established himself as France's leading film scholar and the first to seriously apply the tenets of structuralism as part of a systematic study of cinema. In many ways Metz was emblematic of French theory's growing influence. He had trained under Barthes at the *École Pratique des Hautes Études*, published several of his major essays in the school's academic journal *Communications*, and generally developed his theoretical interests in concert with the larger intellectual movements of the period. At the same time, Metz did more than simply take up film as an occasion to apply structuralist principles. Throughout his work, Metz expressed a deep knowledge of film history and aesthetics as well as a familiarity with predecessors ranging from André Bazin to Edgar Morin and Jean Mitry. He was also very aware of his status as a film theoretician. This marked an important departure from the group of theorists discussed in the previous chapter and even many of the post-war writers at journals like *Cahiers* who continued to think about their task in terms of criticism. Metz, in this respect, inaugurated the end of film study as an informal activity. And, as film study transitioned to a more scholarly enterprise, his engagement with linguistics, structural analysis, and psychoanalysis provided it with a compendium of analytical tools as well as an appreciation for the rigors of formal scholarship.

Metz began this undertaking by considering the relationship between cinema and language. As noted in Chapter 1, early theorists like Vachel Lindsay and Sergei Eisenstein had expressed enthusiasm for certain similarities between the two. Others like Alexandre Astruc, who equated the camera with a writing utensil in his term *caméra-stylo*, and Raymond Spottiswoode developed their own subsequent formulations.[13] But, for the most part, the exact nature of this relationship remained unclear. Metz set out to produce a more definitive verdict, and in short order, he proceeded to reject the basic analogy between cinema and language. First, he noted that film is a one-way form of communication. It presents a complete message to an audience that has no opportunity to directly respond. Film is thus divorced from the dialogical component of language. Second, there is no way to isolate film's smallest discrete unit. Language consists of letters and words, both of which can be combined to create larger units of meaning, the basis for something also known as double articulation. Although there are some similarities between these linguistic units and film's smallest unit (i.e., the individual shot), these corollaries are imprecise and do not hold up to sustained scrutiny. The cinematic image, for instance, is produced on a basis of visual resemblance meaning that it is motivated, not arbitrary as in the case of letter and words. Also, there is no limit to the number of images that can be produced, meaning that images cannot be reduced to a fixed system in the way that words can be reduced to the finite number of letters that make up the alphabet. In this regard, the individual shot functions more like a statement. It says "here is a cat," rather than just "cat." And while most shots feature a large amount of information, often containing more than one just one statement, they are also already determined by the filmmaker. Thus certain meanings are more actively shaped by the filmmaker's choices than by binary oppositions as in a purely linguistic situation.

Despite making an ample case for why film differs from language, Metz does not entirely dismiss the analogy. On the contrary, he essentially reformulates the question. In the essay "Some Points in the Semiotics of the Cinema," he writes that "cinema is certainly not a language system (*langue*)." However, it can be considered "a *language*, to the extent that it orders signifying elements within ordered arrangements different from those of spoken idioms" (*Film Language* 105). Here Metz applies a subtle distinction introduced by Ferdinand de Saussure that has been a source of confusion due to an unclear translation. In *Course in General Linguistics*, Saussure uses the term *language* as a classification that includes both *langue* and *parole*, and that therefore designates a broader notion of language as a human faculty or aptitude (but which has been variously translated either as "human speech" or, like *langue*, simply as "language").[14] As Metz further explains it, *langue* specifies the rules and procedures within a particular language but which cannot explain all of the variations that can occur as part of that language as a whole. In this regard, Metz views cinema as a language that is without, or that cannot be reduced to, an exact *langue*. As part of his argument, then, cinema necessitates a departure from linguistics in any kind of strict sense and, more specifically, marks a shift away from focusing on either minimal units of signification or the regulative structures that restrict the possible combinations between units. Insofar as narrative cinema is organized around distinct formal conventions, it nevertheless retains an organizational logic that is tantamount to a kind of syntax or grammar. It is in this way that the methods associated with linguistics are still useful.

In drawing this distinction, Metz goes on to consider the syntagmatic organization of film or, rather, the ordering of images into sequential units that then serve to structure cinema as a narrative discourse. In particular, he identifies several different types of segments, or signifying units, within conventional editing patterns. The "alternating syntagm," for instance, refers to the combination of individual shots to signify either simultaneous action within a unified space or concurrent actions across different spatial relations. Metz subsequently constructs a more expansive taxonomy, known as the ***grande syntagmatique***, consisting of eight different sequential models. Although there is no necessary limit to the ways in which images can be arranged, these models highlight how cinema has given rise to a relatively small number of narrative conventions, organizational patterns that signify generic formulas and to which both filmmakers and viewers have become accustomed. Over time, and as a matter of "repetition over innumerable films," these units gradually become "more or less fixed" though never entirely "immutable" (*Film Language* 101). In other words, they function in a programmatic sense, establishing certain protocols or guidelines rather than a set of restrictive rules. Metz adopted the term **code** as a way to distinguish this function from *langue*—which remains in his view a more rigid and systematic set of regulations—and to escape the more prescriptive approach of linguistics proper. While the new term served to sidestep some of the ambiguity within Saussure's earlier account, it was not without questions of its own. Following Metz's introduction of the term, Italian semiotician Umberto Eco and film-maker Pier Paolo Pasolini further debated the nature of codes and their exact function within cinema. Though these debates some-times resulted in an impasse, they also exhibited a new theoretical intensity. Like earlier debates between formalism and realism, these exchanges were vital in raising the intellectual stakes for a still devel-oping body of scholarship.

By shifting the focus away from the strict equation between lan-guage and cinema, Metz reoriented the priorities of film analysis. Whereas linguistics aims to identify general rules, ones that remain in effect without reference to specific instances, cinema necessitates a different approach. For Metz, structural analysis can be applied to specific examples to discern the way in which different sub-codes interact and how these configurations participate as part of more general cinematic or cultural codes. This in turn requires a dual per-spective. Following the work that began with his account of the *grande syntagmatique*, Metz establishes the importance of analyzing film's formal components and the ability to detail their cinematic specificity. Meanwhile, in *Language and Cinema*, the book that fol-lowed his collection of earlier essays, Metz indicates that analysis aims to elucidate "the structure of [a particular] text, and not the text itself." This is necessary precisely since the structuring system as such "is never directly attested" (*Language and Cinema* 73). In general, Metz advanced a series of issues that demanded more sophisticated, and critical, modes of analysis. Even though his own methods fluc-tuated, his efforts established a rapport between film analysis and important semioticians like Roland Barthes and Julia Kristeva. His focus on narrative discourse also recalled the work of narratologists and literary theorists like Gérard Genette and Tzvetan Todorov. In this regard, he also played a critical role in introducing the underpin-nings of **close analysis**. This refers to a type of textual engagement often involving shot-by-shot analysis and can be seen in the con-tributions of Thierry Kuntzel, Marie-Claire Ropars-Wuilleumier, and, most notably, Raymond Bellour. Bellour is best known for his incredibly meticulous breakdown of works by Alfred Hitchcock and other popular Hollywood directors. This type of analysis is also evident in later works like the *Cahiers* editorial piece on *Young Mr. Lincoln* (1939) and in Stephen Heath's lengthy analysis of *Touch of Evil* (1958). In contrast to Metz's earliest forays, these later works balanced semiotics' microscopic attention to individual parts with broader considerations of how film form is inextricably intertwined in larger ideological meanings.

In the mid–1970s, Metz undertook a major new direction with *The Imaginary Signifier*. This study extended his earlier exploration of film and language by introducing a wide-ranging application of psychoanalytic theory. The most important part of this new approach is that Metz considers cinematic spectatorship, something that had been entirely absent in his earlier work. As a result of this turn to psychoanalysis, Metz specifically posits a spectator based on Freud and Lacan's model of the individual subject. In this respect, it is important to note that the spectator often refers to a certain position rather than actual audience members. More specifically, this is the position that the film itself constructs for the viewer. While this means that this approach is largely a matter of speculation, Metz uses it as a premise to consider the role of unconscious desires in cinema's appeal to its hypothetical viewer. This allows him to introduce additional concepts like voyeurism, fetishism, and disavowal.

This same logic informs his even more significant account of **identification**. Stemming primarily from Lacan's account of the mirror stage but also in line with the work of subsequent theorists like Baudry, Metz holds that the screen presents the spectator with an imaginary visual field that the spectator then identifies with. Metz adds an important distinction, however, in dividing identification between primary and secondary variations. In the first, the spectator identifies with whatever the camera sees. The viewer perceives images as though he or she is the source that determines that which is seen. In secondary identification, the spectator identifies with a character within the film. This typically means that the viewer identifies with the character that comes closest to his or her own social position. Finally, in the last section of *The Imaginary Signifier*, Metz reconsiders the categories of metaphor and metonymy as developed by Roman Jakobson and Lacan. These categories, and their corollaries displacement and condensation, function somewhat similarly to the sequential units that made up the *grande syntagmatique*,

But instead of simply distinguishing spatial and temporal relations, metaphor and metonym are understood as resembling the complex figures or tropes associated with the logic of dreams and examples of psychopathology. Although the material Metz explored in *The Imaginary Signifier* represented a significant shift from his earlier interests, there is a tendency to treat it all as part of a cohesive larger project sometimes labeled "cine-semiology" or "cine-structuralism."

In sum, Metz played a decisive role in establishing film theory as a more rigorous and distinctive practice. His semiotic and narrative analyses, his consideration of psychoanalysis, and his affiliation with the general tenets of structuralism provided film study with a much stronger intellectual foundation. This provided it with the traction it needed to resonate with more serious scholars. And as part of these developments, Metz initiated the larger institutional shift that was equally important in facilitating subsequent theoretical inquiry.[15] Whereas state-sponsored institutions like the Moscow Film School or France's *L'Insitute des hautes etudes cinématographiques* (Institute for Advanced Cinemagraphic Study, abbreviated as IDHEC) had been the primary basis for scholarly work, Metz began the process of assimilating it into the university system. In some respects, this marked the formal recognition of film as a serious object of study, completing the work that had begun decades earlier with the likes of Lindsay and Münsterberg. But it was not just that film warranted serious consideration because of its aesthetic merits as early theorists had imagined. It warranted consideration because of its larger social and cultural implications, and because of its ability to illustrate the pertinence of contemporaneous theoretical concerns.

MAY 1968 AND AFTERWARD

As mentioned at the beginning of this chapter, there were several divergent, even contradictory, developments in the period that followed World War II. In the United States, for example, the 1950s became known as a period of affluence and conspicuous consumption, with the idyllic suburban families depicted on television programs like *Father Knows Best* serving as the era's defining representatives. At the same time, this period saw the beginning of several clashes that continued to escalate into the following decade.

The Civil Rights Movement began to take shape and established a fundamental prototype for the New Left. Youth culture emerged in conjunction with new forms of popular culture—dynamic new genres like rock and roll that blended growing commercial appeal with adolescent rebellion. There was also an expanding counter-culture, with groups like the Beats and other bohemians who pursued different forms of artistic and social experimentation in cities like New York and San Francisco. By the end of the 1950s, these developments began to have a palpable impact on college campuses across America and in the concurrent revitalization of grassroots film cultures. Both campus film societies and the independent groups devoted to alternative forms of production and exhibition adopted certain aspects of the oppositional rhetoric that was emerging at this time. Embracing new forms of international and avant-garde cinema that challenged Hollywood's status quo was quickly becoming a bold anti-establishment statement.

In many ways, May 1968 represents a culmination of the political consciousness and growing opposition that intensified significantly in this period. The Civil Rights Movement by that time had merged with the more radical attitudes of the Black Power Movement in general and the explicitly confrontational tactics of the Black Panther Party in particular. Student groups and the New Left were further radicalized as the Vietnam War continued to escalate and as the hypocrisy of Western imperialism became blatantly apparent. Student demonstrations became openly virulent and the authorities' treatment of protestors, for instance at the Democratic National Convention in Chicago that year, became excessively brutal. In the case of France, the events that took place throughout May and early June epitomized a decade of upheaval and the general state of crisis that had come to preoccupy much of the West. As with earlier movements, the May protests in France began with student demonstrations but quickly escalated into something more. As students from Nanterre University, a new university built in the early 1960s outside of Paris, joined with students at the Sorbonne in the heart of the city's Latin Quarter, the protestors shut down the school and demanded a more active role in shaping the conditions of higher education. The French government brought in the riot police to remove the students, which led to a series of violent confrontations. In the days that followed, teachers, workers, and many others joined the protestors in massive strikes that shut down the entire country.

The May protests were climactic. They brought together most all of the grievances that had been brewing for over a decade and they did so on a scale that briefly brought France to the brink of collapse. But as the government orchestrated several compromises—offering deals to appease the major trade unions and the PCF—many were left dissatisfied. While many participants saw 1968 as the beginning of a decline and a turning away from direct political activism, it marked a different kind of turning point for French film culture. As Sylvia Harvey notes in her detailed account, the May protests made radical politics a ubiquitous topic for filmmakers, for editorial boards at film journals, and for a burgeoning generation of film theorists.

There were several, somewhat subtle, precursors to this politicization. The film community quickly mobilized in protest, for example, when the government attempted to oust Henri Langlois, the influential and popular head of Paris' *Cinématheque*.[16] There was another important model in avant-garde groups like the Situationists and the writers associated with *Tel Quel*.[17] Both groups blended theory with politics and aesthetics to form what **D. N. Rodowick** later defined as **political modernism**, or, more specifically, the "desire to combine semiotic and ideological analysis with the development of an avant-garde aesthetic practice dedicated to the production of radical social effects" (*Crisis of Political Modernism* 1–2).

This same development was also evident in the work of Jean Luc Godard and Chris Marker, two of the French new wave's most prominent and accomplished filmmakers. Both had always been known for experimenting with film's formal conventions, but over the course of the 1960s they became more radical in demystifying the means of cinematic production. In films such as *Week-end* (1967) and *Joyful Knowledge* (1969), Godard, for example, interjected explicit theoretical and political references as part of a self-reflexive campaign to deconstruct the relationship between image and viewer. By the end of the decade, both Godard and Marker were working as members of different filmmaking collectives—the Dziga Vertov group and SLON (*Société pour le lancement des oeuvres nouvelles*

[Society for the Promotion of New Works], which later adopted the name Medvedkine) respectively. These groups were an attempt to re-organize the existing mode of production. They aimed to desta-bilize the standard divisions in labor while also encouraging more communal forms of filmmaking. These groups viewed themselves as a militant vanguard and used theory as an important weapon in its attack on bourgeois aesthetics.

The editors at *Cahiers du cinéma* eventually followed this same tra-jectory. Although some of the new wave filmmakers associated with the journal had introduced a spirit of rebellion, *Cahiers* had none-theless maintained a predominantly appreciative tone in its criticism. Starting with the Langlois affair, however, the journal began paying closer attention to the intersections between film and politics. The events of May then prompted a more significant change in its overall position.

In the Fall 1969 issue of *Cahiers*, editors Jean-Louis Comolli and Jean Narboni issued a statement they titled "Cinema/Ideology/ Criticism." In it, they state that it is imperative to establish "a clear theoretical base" to define the journal's critical objectives in the field of cinema ("Cinema/Ideology/Criticism" 27). Their main point in what follows is that film is part of the larger economic system of capitalism and, as such, it is also "part of the ideological system" ("Cinema/Ideology/Criticism" 28). The job of critics is to under-stand how films are part of that system and to ultimately change the conditions of that system. Comolli and Narboni then outline seven different types of films. The largest category consists of films that are "imbued through and through with the dominant ideology" ("Cinema/Ideology/Criticism" 30). A different category includes films that attack ideology through both form and content while another includes films that are politically progressive but very con-ventional in form.

Their most interesting category concerns "films which seem at first sight to belong firmly within the [dominant] ideology and to be completely under its sway, but which turn out to be so only in an ambiguous manner" ("Cinema/Ideology/Criticism" 34). Comolli and Narboni elaborate further that in this fifth category of their taxonomy, "An internal criticism is taking place which cracks the film apart at the seams. If one reads the film obliquely, looking for symptoms; if one looks beyond its apparent formal coherence, one can see that it is riddled with cracks: it is splitting under an internal tension which is simply not there in an ideologically innocuous film" ("Cinema/Ideology/Criticism" 34). These categories and the document as a whole went a long way in establishing an agenda for the generation of film theorists that followed in the aftermath of May 1968. Indeed, these later theorists were devoted to either critiquing films as evidence of the dominant ideology or outlining the parameters for a new form of filmmaking capable of combating the dominant ideology. They were also repeatedly drawn to the problem posed by Comolli and Narboni's fifth category: films that were both complicit with the Hollywood system of production and yet inimical to its governing logic. Film theorists were drawn to these paradoxical instances because they exemplified the contradictions incumbent within modern society and because French theory provided them with the tools that were specifically designed to address such complexities. In the immediate aftermath of May 1968, *Cahiers*, together with like-minded French journals *Positif* and *Cinéthique*, provided an initial platform for critics to take up Comolli and Narboni's call to action. More generally, however, this task fell to a new generation of scholars as film theory relocated to the Anglophone academy in the 1970s.

SUMMARY

Film theory began a dramatic turn in the middle of the twentieth century. This new approach took root in France with the emergence of structuralism and several related theoretical frameworks (i.e. semiotics, psychoanalysis, and Marxism). Key theorists like Roland Barthes, Jacques Lacan, and Louis Althusser played critical roles in introducing new terms and analytical techniques as part of this larger movement. By the early 1960s, Christian Metz and others had begun applying these terms to cinema, advancing the overall rigor and sophistication of film analysis. French theory as a whole represents a broader transition whereby intellectuals and scholars became more politically engaged. Amidst a background of protest and radical politics, they began questioning social and academic conventions.

Questions

1. What prompted the turn to structuralism? What are the challenges of applying its different methods to film?

2. How does psychoanalysis define the subject? How is this definition relevant to film theorists?

3. Why do film theorists become interested in different social dynamics? How does film serve to naturalize the role of power within certain social relationships?

4. How did the social and political context of the 1960s contribute to the direction of film theory? How did these factors specifically impact earlier vestiges of film culture, for instance journals like *Cahiers du cinéma*?

5. In what ways does French theory represent a major turning point away from the film theorists discussed in Chapter 1? Are there any points of overlap? If not, why did film theory experience such a sudden and drastic shift in focus?

NOTES

1 As Simon Clarke (1981) explains it, "Lévi-Strauss' achievement is to isolate an autonomous order of reality, the symbolic order, which exists independently of the things that are symbolized and the people who symbolize. Cultural meanings are inherent in the symbolic order and these meanings are independent of, and prior to, the external world, on the one hand, and human subjects, on the other. Thus the world only has an objective existence in the symbolic orders that represent it" (2). The objective status of this order was important in several respects—it fortified the social scientific basis of structuralism, distinguishing its explanatory power as more critical than extant models. See also Dosse (1997), Gutting (2001), Kauppi (1996, 2010), and Lotringer and Cohen (2001) for overviews of the rise of structuralism in relation to French intellectual life.

2 See Doss (1997): 22–3 and Roudinesco (1997): 275–6.

3 Included in Barthes (1977).

4 See, for example, Bergstrom (1999) and Williams (1981).

5 These writings are included in Donald, Friedberg, and Marcus (1998).

6 Roudinesco (1997) and Macey (1988) provide further details of these intellectual influences.

7 See Anthony Wilden's commentary in Lacan (1968): 274–5, and the transla-
tor note in Lacan (2002): 335. Silverman (1983) provides an extensive overview of this concept and its adoption by film theorists.

8 See Dayan (1976), Stephen Heath's *Questions of Cinema* (1981), and Silverman
(1983). Žižek makes various references to this process throughout his work.
His most sustained consideration can be found in *The Fright of Real Tears*
(2001).

9 See Dosse (1996): 273–83, Kauppi (1996): 109–25, and Rodowick (1994):
5–35.

10 See Debord (1995).

11 See Turner (1990).

12 See Hall, Hobson, Lowe, and Willis (1996).

13 Astruc's essay "The Birth of a New Avant-Garde: *La Caméra-Stylo*" is
included in Graham and Vindendeau (2009).

14 See Sanders (2004): 4–5.

15 D. N. Rodowick addresses this transition in *Elegy for Theory* (2014); see especially 131–52.

16 See Harvey (1980): 14–27.

17 The Situationists were an avant-garde group associated with Guy Debord.
They shared certain similarities with the Surrealists and Dadaists. See Home
(1996).

SCREEN THEORY, 1969–96

With the structuralist and post-structuralist challenge to the intellectual establishment, film theory had a model that set the terms and
tone for its rapid ascent in the decades that followed. As film study
was assimilated into the Anglo-American academy, its theoretical
interests continued to move away from the medium's aesthetic status
and questions surrounding authorship. Although these concerns had
played a decisive role in establishing film's merit and in elevating
earlier forms of film criticism, film theory throughout the 1970s
and 1980s drew upon French theory and the specific developments
associated with semiotics, psychoanalysis, and Marxism to shift its
focus more fully to deconstructing cinema and its ideological functions. This direction also marked a continuation of political modernism or, rather, the view that theory was coextensive with political
and aesthetic intervention. As such, film study took root within the
academy and gained formal recognition as an inter-disciplinary and
critical approach to analyzing culture and society. This field quickly
became a general breeding ground for lively intellectual debate and
innovative theoretical inquiry.

The development of film theory at this time was significantly
enhanced by the emergence of several important journals. Although
the British journal *Screen* was the most prominent of these, others

like *Jump Cut*, *Camera Obscura*, and *October* were equally representative of the general theoretical ferment that developed during this
period. These outlets were of course an invaluable resource. They
provided individual theorists with a platform while also facilitating both debate and dialogue between different theoretical positions. In this respect, they not only served to fortify a still fledgling
academic discipline but also brokered the gap between the field's
new scholarly ambitions and its ties to earlier forms of film culture. In addition to publishing the work of contemporary theorists,
for instance, these journals further contributed by commissioning
translations, coordinating festivals, conferences, and workshops,
and debating pedagogical issues related to teaching film and media.
In this regard, Screen Theory, similar to the designation of French
theory, is more a matter of convenience than a fixed body of
knowledge. It refers to the flurry of theoretical activity that took
place at this time and the general concerns that took precedence at
Screen and similar journals.

As one common point of interest, film theory during the 1970s
and 1980s became increasingly concerned with the relationship
between moving images and socially structured forms of inequity.
This entailed drawing further attention to film as a complex system
of representation and to how its specific formal techniques reinforce the dominant ideology. It was on this basis, for example, that
feminist theorists developed a more critical account of how patriarchy structures images of women. Post-colonial theorists similarly
went on to interrogate the role of Euro-centrism and the history of
colonial rule in structuring the images of racial and ethnic minorities. Queer theorists, in turn, questioned the pervasiveness of het-
erosexuality in shaping the form and function of desire. By the end
of the 1980s, many of these questions coalesced in post-modern
theory's more general efforts to destabilize Western thought. While
there were important intersections as these distinct movements all
sought to radicalize academic inquiry, there was also disagreement
and criticism directed at these developments. Some of these issues
are discussed here, but for the most part they are addressed in the following chapter. These disagreements are an important reminder that
as much as film theory advanced in this period, it was still in many
ways an intellectual practice in transition.

SCREEN AND THEORY

The British journal *Screen* illustrates not only the dramatic transition that took place in film theory in the 1970s but also the development of film study more generally. While *Screen* was officially founded in 1969, it was the outgrowth of a long-term grassroots campaign that began in 1950 "to encourage the use of film as a visual aid in formal education."[1] In this regard, the journal was rooted in many of the same principles that had guided earlier theorists in their efforts to legitimize film. Unlike many of the state-sponsored institutions that emerged as an extension of these efforts, however, the Society for Education in Film and Television (SEFT) did not focus on film production or the development of technical skills. Instead it was a volunteer-based organization that consisted mainly of primary and secondary school teachers. To best serve its members, SEFT devoted much of its attention to various publications. These included several instructional guidebooks and starting in 1959 a bi-monthly supplement titled *Screen Education*. Throughout most of its first two decades, SEFT remained closely aligned with and, for all intents and purposes, financially dependent on the British Film Institute's Educational Department. Nevertheless, the organization was also afforded some degree of autonomy.

This was a key factor when in 1969, amidst fluctuations in its leadership, SEFT decided to discontinue *Screen Education* and replace it with *Screen*. The editors announced that the new journal would "provide a forum in which controversial areas relevant to the study of film and television can be examined and argued," at the same time cautioning that "It is by no means clear what the nature of Film Study should be."[2] Despite this initial uncertainty, *Screen* quickly took up the task of shaping this new field and, with the appointment of Sam Rohdie as editor, asserted its commitment "to the development of theoretical ideas and more systematic methods of study."[3] As part of his inaugural editorial, Rohdie further clarified this position in relationship to SEFT's earlier focus on educational issues: "*Screen* will aim to go beyond subjective taste-ridden criticism and try to develop more systematic approaches over a wider field. [. . .] Above all film must be studied as a new medium, a product of this century and of the machine, and which as a new medium and a new mode of expression challenges traditional notions of art and criticism and the system of education which still in part is tied to these notions."[4] This new approach developed quickly as more scholarly focused contributors like **Peter Wollen** and Ben Brewster joined the journal. Both Wollen and Brewster had been associated with the *New Left Review*, the British publication that had most fully embraced French theory. Additionally, Brewster had translated several of Althusser's key works into English. These associations further confirmed *Screen*'s new direction, signaling both its departure from SEFT's earlier pedagogical concerns and the evaluative criticism that remained the focus at publications like *Movie* and *Sight and Sound*.

Even with *Screen*'s theoretical turn, it continued to pursue a wide variety of interests. This included an entire issue dedicated to the translation of 1920s Soviet avant-garde artists, debates on neorealism, and numerous engagements with the work of Bertolt Brecht.[5] This heterogeneity makes it difficult to reduce *Screen* to a single position or doctrine. However, it is possible to identify three general interests that came to characterize the journal's direction in the 1970s. First, *Screen* was committed to deepening the association between film theory and the theoretical developments taking place in France. To this end, it featured commissioned translations of many key French essays. In 1971, for instance, it published Comolli and Narboni's "Cinema/Ideology/Criticism" as part of its new commitment to theory. In 1975, Christian Metz's "The Imaginary Signifier" appeared in the pages of *Screen* concurrently with its original French publication. For the most part, these translations were seen as a direct endorsement of French theory. But this was not always the case. For example, in 1973 *Screen* published an essay by Metz together with an extensive critique of his work by the French journal *Cinéthique*.[6] In this instance, *Screen* was more concerned with fostering debate and representing different viewpoints than with simply affirming Metz in some unqualified sense.

Peter Wollen's *Signs and Meaning* served as something of an extension of this effort. Like *Screen*, he sought to radicalize theory by introducing elements of French theory and the book's third chapter, "The Semiology of Cinema," is credited with introducing many Anglo-American readers to the work of Saussure, Barthes, Jakobson, and Metz. At the same time, however, he made a deliberate attempt to add certain modifications. As part of his discussion of semiotics, for example, Wollen introduces Charles Sanders Peirce and his three-part classification of the sign (i.e., the distinction between icons, indices, and symbols).[7] Wollen then uses this distinction as the basis for his critique of André Bazin. In particular, he argues that Bazin developed an aesthetic "founded upon the indexical character of the photographic image" (*Signs and Meaning* 136). But this is a mistake insofar as cinema combines all three variations of the sign as identified by Peirce. "The great weakness," for Wollen, is that almost everyone who has "written about the cinema" takes one type of sign and makes "it the ground of their aesthetic, the 'essential' dimension [while discarding] the rest. This is to impoverish the cinema" (*Signs and Meaning* 141).

Wollen's intervention had a significant impact. It not only altered Bazin's place within film theory for years to come but also served to illustrate the point that it was not enough to simply distill or apply the insights provided by French theory. Instead, it was necessary to synthesize existing materials while also augmenting them with additional distinctions. These same tactics were evident in other ways throughout *Signs and Meaning*. The first chapter, for instance, posits Sergei Eisenstein as the starting point for any serious consideration of cinema. Although this genealogy differed significantly from more comprehensive historical accounts, it allowed Wollen to suggest an implicit convergence between theory and politics within film aesthetics. This maneuvering is even more pronounced in Wollen's reformulation of auteur theory in the book's second chapter. Here he develops an unlikely combination by joining the proven method of auteur-based criticism with the structuralist analyses of Lévi-Strauss and Barthes. This made for a counter-intuitive hybrid model and shows that film theory was still in a transitional stage. Even amidst efforts to move ahead, there were still instances in which recourse to existing models proved useful.

Stephen Heath is another influential figure associated with *Screen* and its commitment to incorporating French theory. Similar to Wollen's *Signs and Meanings*, his essay, "On Screen, in Frame: Film and Ideology," is particularly representative of this period. Although it did not actually appear in *Screen*, it took on additional significance because, prior to publication, it served as the opening address for the

1975 "International Symposium on Film Theory and Criticism," the first of several major conferences hosted by the University of Wisconsin-Milwaukee's Center for Twentieth Century Studies. It then later appeared as the opening chapter in Heath's collection of essays, *Questions of Cinema.*

In the essay, Heath explores film's relationship to ideology and makes a case for why it is the most important heuristic concept in studying cinema. It not only allows Heath to introduce the likes of Althusser and Lacan, but also provides him with a way to situate film in relation to historical materialism and psychoanalysis more broadly. To this end, Heath begins the essay by highlighting two brief references. In the first reference, Marx likens ideology to a camera obscura, an optical device and early precursor to the camera in which images appear upside down. In the second reference, Freud compares the unconscious to a photographic negative in which the image is again inverted. These references show that film is intertwined in much larger efforts to understand modern phenomena like capitalist relations and bourgeois subjectivity. For Heath, this coincidence further suggests that film marks a merger of these different phenomena. Thus, the analysis of cinema as an ideological practice invites not only consideration of "theoretical issues of a more general scope," but also the ways in which historical materialism and psychoanalysis are necessarily intertwined (*Questions of Cinema* 4).

Heath goes on to consider the two other elements that make up his title. To elaborate what he means by "on screen," he refers to the 1902 Biograph film, *Uncle Josh at the Moving Picture Show.* The title character is a "country bumpkin" who, in the midst of viewing his first motion picture, tries to save the female character within the diegesis. He only succeeds, however, in pulling down the screen, not in stopping the image. For Heath, this illustrates that what transpires on screen is only part of film's ideological illusion. As in the various other formulations of apparatus theory, it is not enough to only dispel the image as such. Instead, it is necessary to consider its material existence: its function within a system of relations. In this respect, film analysis requires an understanding "of a certain historicity of ideological formations and mechanisms in relation to the processes of the production of [the subject and] the symbolic as an order that is intersected by but is not merely reducible to [ideological representations]" (*Questions of Cinema* 6). In another gesture to French theory and Althusser in particular, Heath adds that this consideration cannot address ideology as a strictly rational or logical process. Rather, to move beyond Uncle Josh, it is necessary to analyze the contradictions that help to sustain the dominant ideology and its specific signifying practices.

Whereas "on screen" serves as an occasion to consider the relationship between the cinematic image and the conditions that underlie its production, the formulation "in frame" shifts the focus to how the viewing spectator relates to what is on screen. As part of this discussion, Heath stresses that the frame is a restrictive device, one whereby the subject is "ceaselessly recaptured *for* the film" (*Questions of Cinema* 13). In this regard, Heath equates the composition of the frame with the construction of a narrative framework, and, by extension, the different mechanisms that orient and guide the viewer. On one hand, these techniques situate the viewer as a privileged point of reference, the one around which the story's fictional world is nominally organized. On the other hand, however, these techniques are designed to contain or limit meaning. This is clearest in the way that narrative and formal conventions aim to maintain continuity, manipulating the temporal and spatial relationships between images to ensure an impression of coherence. Framing in this sense is also linked to the suturing operations of cinematic discourse: the process by which the subject is produced within a chain of discourse as "lack," a mere signifier in the field of the Other.[8] To put it another way, the viewer is cut off from the production of meaning and consigned to a particular ideological position. To be "in frame" is to be arrested or fettered, an unsuspecting bystander subsumed by the manipulative logic of a fixed symbolic order.

Like Wollen, Heath endeavors to do more than merely explicate ideology's theoretical value. In this case, Heath's intervention can be seen in some of the different rhetorical strategies he embraces as an extension of his theoretical interests. As Warren Buckland notes in a detailed reassessment of Heath's essay, these strategies are immediately evident in its title. There Heath introduces two spatial prepositions that become important in explaining the relationship between film and ideology. According to Buckland, "on" in the formulation "on screen" establishes "the screen not only as a surface, but also as a support that determines the position of the object placed upon it" (*Film Theory* 94). By contrast, "in frame" draws attention to the "boundary between an interior and exterior space," with an emphasis on containment or limitation (*Film Theory* 94). While the two prepositions suggest an incompatible spatial dynamic, their close proximity within the title—separated only by a comma—suggests that they are in some capacity conjoined. For Buckland, this is by design. To paraphrase, he claims that the title uses the specific terms "screen" and "frame" to explain the general relationship between film and ideology. It is possible to parse the latter relationship only by introducing the former as a basis for understanding its complicated dimensions (*Film Theory* 95). True to Buckland's assessment that it is difficult to separate film and ideology, Heath often appears to conflate rather than clarify the relationship between their different dimensions. For instance, in "Narrative Space," and in clear reference to his earlier formulation, Heath writes that the screen "is at once ground, the surface that supports the projected images, and background, its surface caught up in the cone of light to give the frame of the image. Ground and background are one in the alignment of frame and screen, the 'on screen in frame' that is the basis of the spatial articulations a film will make, the start of its composition" (*Questions of Cinema* 38). In this case, the oscillation between ground and background suggests that ideology both precedes and permeates the cinematic image. It is necessary to recognize that these are different dimensions, but that they are also fundamentally intertwined.

At points like this Heath's theoretical prose takes on a challenging performative quality. This was consistent with *Screen*'s second defining characteristic during this period. In the same way that Comolli and Narboni asserted that film could escape the dominant ideology only by rejecting it both in terms of content and form, many theorists adopted a similar approach to writing. D. N. Rodowick, in his analysis of political modernism, associates this style of writing with ***écriture***, particularly as it came to be practiced by the *Tel Quel* group in the 1960s. This practice, like political modernism more generally, was based on the belief that certain modernist or avant-garde techniques were capable of dissolving the boundary between aesthetic and theoretical work. Following this logic, many theorists adopted an outward hostility to conventional narrative styles and the imperative that all communication function in an instrumental manner. In this regard, language itself was taken to be a site of contestation—an opportunity to challenge the status quo and enact some form of social change. For many readers, this style of writing renders theory inaccessible. This continues to constitute one of the main objections directed against theory. Several members of *Screen*'s editorial board even resigned their position in 1976, issuing a statement in which they cited the journal's difficult prose as a severe handicap. The remaining board members defended the journal's complex terminology, but they did so mainly on practical grounds (i.e., as part of the challenge of assimilating French theory) rather than acknowledging it as a strategic intervention designed to usurp rational discourse.

As an extension of this tenet, several theorists simultaneously advocated for a **counter-cinema**, an oppositional style of film-making that would serve to expand *Screen*'s critique of the dominant ideology. To some degree, these calls were indebted to the model provided by Soviet montage filmmakers like Eisenstein and Vertov. They were also based on more contemporary examples like Newsreel, an American vanguard group that made agit-prop style films as part of their political activism. As a practice, counter-cinema simultaneously recalled the work of other avant-garde groups like the structuralist/materialist filmmakers who borrowed certain theoretical ideas in their rejection of orthodox film aesthetics. While these different examples all contributed to the general principle of counter-cinema, Peter Wollen developed a more programmatic set of guidelines. In some ways, these guidelines were explicitly doctrinaire. For example, Wollen drew a schematic distinction between the "deadly sins" of mainstream Hollywood cinema and the "cardinal virtues" of his proposed counter-cinema. Although he repeatedly cites the work of Jean Luc Godard to exemplify the virtues of counter-cinema, his general distinction implies a more rudimentary binary logic,[9] the implication being that it is possible to dismantle Hollywood by replacing its conventions with a different set of conventions. For instance, adopting a strategy of narrative disruption promised to erase the deleterious effects of narrative continuity. Wollen further supported his policy with references to Bertolt Brecht. Foregrounding techniques like direct address, parody, and asynchronous sound were all ways of laying bare the means of cinematic production. They further promised to mobilize the viewer against the standard pleasures of Hollywood entertainment.

While these calls for a counter-cinema were the logical extension of *Screen*'s theoretical platform, they were not without certain ironies. One result was that *Screen* formed a new echelon of canonical filmmakers. In addition to Godard and precursors like Eisenstein, this list included Nagisa Oshima, Glauber Rocha, Jean-Marie Straub and Danièle Huillet. Though these filmmakers certainly represented an important departure from standard narrative cinema, their appraisal was often reminiscent of the auteur-criticism that *Screen*'s theorists had ostensibly rejected. Another irony was that the calls for a counter-cinema were couched within new hierarchies. For example, Wollen, in his essay "The Two Avant-Gardes," draws a distinction between filmmakers like Godard, who he endorses, and a second group that he associates with the Co-Op movement in Britain and New American Cinema more generally. Wollen criticizes this second group for its excessive formalism—its recourse to abstraction, its aversion to language, and what he considers to be its solipsistic self-reflexivity. In his view, this group had regressed into a kind of Romanticism. They pursued art for art's sake and their only interest was to locate cinema's purist form. As a result, these groups "ended up sharing many preoccupations in common with its worst enemies," by which Wollen means André Bazin (*Readings and Writings* 97). Accordingly, he finds that most avant-garde filmmakers had returned to a kind of ontological commitment to cinema rather than a rigorous materialist critique of it. Though not without its merits, Wollen's critique nonetheless extended the same binary logic that informed his prescriptive instructions for counter-cinema and his earlier attack on Bazin. In both cases, film theory became a matter of pitting good objects against bad objects. As productive as this was in providing film theory with a series of inaugural rallying points, this mentality gave way to animosity and fatigue, eventually draining much of the vibrancy that distinguished *Screen* throughout the 1970s.

Screen's third area of focus developed in close conjunction with its commitment to French theory and its interest in developing a counter-cinema. As part of both of these interests, many of the journal's contributors were engaged in developing more detailed models of critical textual analysis. These models were indebted to earlier examples like the *Cahiers du cinéma* text on John Ford's *Young Mr. Lincoln*, which *Screen* published in 1972. These models continued to increase in sophistication as Raymond Bellour's work began to appear in English and with Stephen Heath's ongoing work on enunciation and subject positioning. These analyses were largely devoted to dominant cinema, which was generally equated with Hollywood. While it was fairly clear what constituted Hollywood cinema at this point, there were still debates regarding some of its nuances. It was in this regard that **Colin MacCabe** provided a useful distinction with what he labeled the classic realist text. The purpose of these models was twofold. On one hand, their primary objective was to fully understand and then deconstruct dominant cinema and its operations. On the other hand, this understanding provided a better foundation for developing a more effective counter-cinema.

In terms of distinguishing the textual basis of realism, MacCabe emphasizes film's discursive operation. This shifts the analytical focus to narrative discourse more broadly and draws greater attention to the intersections between film and literature. This designation also serves to move critical analysis away from questions of medium specificity. In this regard, MacCabe suggests that realism is not located within the image at an ontological or empirical level. Instead, realism is something that is discursively constructed through a specific set of textual operations. As an extension of this new focus, MacCabe also indicates the importance of discerning a hierarchy of operations within a given text. Although he does not directly refer to Roland Barthes' *S/Z*, MacCabe's approach is clearly indebted to this particular type of advanced structuralist analysis.[10] For instance, in *S/Z*, Barthes identifies five specific codes as part of his interpretation of a classic realist text (i.e., Honoré de Balzac's short story "Sarrasine"). More specifically, Barthes shows how such texts allow for moments of indeterminacy, excess, and transgression. These elements are permitted, however, only insofar as they are orchestrated in a way that their disruptive force is ultimately contained.

To illustrate this approach with respect to cinema, MacCabe provides a brief analysis of *American Graffiti* (1973). The film follows two teenagers the night before they are supposed to leave for college in a kind of condensed coming-of-age story. One of the teenage boys,

Curt Henderson (Richard Dreyfuss), is confronted by an alluring unknown woman who, in MacCabe's account, engenders a temporary crisis of self-questioning. Much of the remaining movie then follows Curt in his attempt to "refind an origin which can function as a guarantee of identity" ("Theory and Film" 18). This quest culminates when Curt arrives at the local radio station and encounters the elusive disc jockey (Wolfman Jack) whose voice permeates the film's soundtrack. This is the film's most decisive moment for several reasons. First, it provides narrative closure by signaling the moment Curt overcomes the uncertainty introduced by the mysterious woman. MacCabe characterizes this as the moment at which Curt locates a proper father figure, suggesting that the narrative is couched in oedipal overtones. At the same time, and more importantly, the final scene reinforces this development by bringing together two discursive orders (e.g. the sound track and the image track) that the film has otherwise endeavored to keep separate. As MacCabe explains it: "For everyone else Wolfman Jack is a name which finds its reality only in the differential world of sound but Curt is able to reunite name and bearer so that a full presence can provide the certainty of what he is and what he must do" ("Theory and Film" 19). In other words, the film hinges on its ability to manipulate the sound–image hierarchy, along with the relationships between other discursive operations, to produce a coherent, ostensibly pleasurable, narrative resolution.

As mentioned earlier, this approach marks a shift away from earlier concerns regarding film's aesthetic or ontological status. In the effort to develop more rigorous forms of analysis, theorists at *Screen* and elsewhere became increasingly aware that film's ideological function was not limited to one particular property. Instead, it was tied to a complex system of interrelated discursive and textual operations. This meant that there was no clear benefit to condemning film's affinity for realism. As with many of its features, film's realistic quality can be used either in the service of dominant ideology or as part of a militant counter-cinema. The more important task for theorists is to delineate when and how certain discursive operations naturalize or enforce one particular set of cultural values. To this end, MacCabe's specific example highlights the growing concern for sound as an important, and often neglected, discursive component. The final scene in *American Graffiti* certainly foreshadows French theorist **Michel Chion**'s later and more detailed analysis of sound's importance. In particular, the disc jockey figure recalls his concept of the ***acousmêtre***, a character within the diegesis who speaks while remaining unseen. For Chion, these figures often hold a disproportionate degree of power and the moment that voice and body finally come together is always highly charged.

The 1970s were an incredibly productive period for *Screen* and film theory in general. Although *Screen* and several similar journals allowed individual theorists to pursue a wide variety of interests at this time, there were also a number of common threads. There was, for instance, a concerted effort to incorporate the insights furnished by French theory. This involved synthesizing and in some cases revising these insights as part of these theorists' own efforts to critique film's ideological functions. The development of this general foundation coincided with calls for a counter-cinema and the emergence of more nuanced methods of analysis. Both of these interests marked a continuation of political modernism and the belief that theoretical work had a distinct political valence. Several of the theorists at *Screen*, for example, considered their work to be part of a challenge against existing intellectual practices.

While many of these threads would continue to develop in the decades that followed, much of the work carried out at *Screen* would also become absorbed into film study's basic idiom. For example, MacCabe's classic realist text served in some capacity as the basis for later accounts of the more general distinction, classical Hollywood cinema. Following the subsequent scholarship of **David Bordwell** and others, this latter term provided a more thorough framework for analyzing narrative cinema's formal practices. As the theoretical innovations of the 1970s were integrated into a more formalized academic rubric, there was a tendency to minimize or erase the political overtones that were once an important influence. This set the stage for a growing antagonism that is more fully examined in the first section of Chapter 4.

FEMINIST FILM THEORY

Feminist film theory quickly became the most distinctive and important innovation in film theory's overall growth during the 1970s. While it emerged alongside the shifting theoretical interests taking root at journals like *Screen*, it also instilled these general developments with a more pronounced sense of focus and urgency. In particular, feminist film theory drew upon psychoanalysis to demonstrate how patriarchal ideology structures visual representations of sexual difference and gender. This provided film study with an incredibly powerful framework for critical analysis and immediately prompted further debate and inquiry. In addition to its direct impact on film as a scholarly field, feminist film theory was important because of its ties to feminism as a broader social and political movement. In this regard, it not only introduced significant theoretical insights but also provided a more prominent case in which theorization was intertwined with other critical endeavors. The success of feminist film theory established a model that other new areas like post-colonial theory and queer theory would soon follow.

As an extension of a broader political struggle, feminist film theory brought together an especially diverse set of influences. These included earlier feminist theorists like Simone de Beauvoir as well as contemporaries like Kate Millet and Juliet Mitchell. As a movement, Betty Friedan's *The Feminine Mystique* served as an important catalyst in launching what became feminism's second wave. Another factor in shaping these developments was the fact that women's liberation had been relegated to a secondary status within even the most radical leftist groups of the 1960s.[11] This illustrated the degree to which patriarchy remained firmly entrenched and compelled feminist groups to explore more extreme viewpoints. As a sub-field within film study, feminist film theorists drew upon these influences together with the ideas provided by French theory and the work being done at *Screen*. Their inaugural efforts were also informed by the recent contributions of film critics like Molly Haskell and Marjorie Rosen. Both Haskell and Rosen had adopted a more sociological approach in which they mainly described or categorized the stereotypical roles within Hollywood cinema. Although this work was important in that it was among the first to address the relationship between women and representation, it was also uncritical in most of its assessments.

Claire Johnston noted the limitations of this type of criticism in a series of essays in *Screen* and the supplemental pamphlet *Notes on Women's Cinema*, also published by SEFT. In doing so, Johnston began the preliminary work of establishing a more critical and theoretically informed feminist approach. This initial intervention was quickly followed by what became a decisive turning point: **Laura Mulvey**'s incomparable essay, "Visual Pleasure and Narrative Cinema." Although it is one of the most widely referenced theoretical texts in all of the humanities, it is still worth recounting in some detail to fully appreciate its immense impact. Part of what immediately distinguishes the essay is its tone. Mulvey is blunt and uncompromising in stating her method and her primary thesis: "Psychoanalytic theory is thus appropriated here as a political weapon, demonstrating the way the unconscious of patriarchal society has structured film form" (*Feminist Film Theory* 58). She is similarly adamant in announcing her over-all mission: "It is said that analyzing pleasure, or beauty, destroys it. That is the intention of this article" (*Feminist Film Theory* 60). This call for a "total negation" of the existing system was more direct and aggressive than even the most severe critiques put forward by her colleagues at *Screen*. Mulvey's polemical rhetoric thus promptly distinguished the feminist outlook as one of the most radical factions within film theory.

While Mulvey's manifesto-like call to action was an important part of the essay, most of the document is devoted to analyzing the paradoxical role of women in Hollywood cinema. In this regard, Mulvey begins with the premise that women are relegated to a sub-servient position within most narrative cinema. This adheres to de Beauvoir's general premise that woman is Other, meaning that she is consigned to secondary social status and considered subordinate to man's privileged place as the universal subject. It also follows Johnston's assertion that "The image of the woman becomes merely the trace of the exclusion and repression of Woman" (*Feminist Film Theory* 34). Yet Mulvey notes that there is a discrepancy between this subordinate position and woman's overall function. It is in this respect that she draws attention to the issue of visual pleasure. Narrative cinema is organized around its ability to engender differ-ent types of pleasure. One type concerns scopophilia, or the gen-eral pleasure of looking. This phenomenon also takes a more acute form in **voyeurism**: the desire to see others, particularly something forbidden, while remaining unseen. Cinema is also associated with a narcissistic pleasure. Here Mulvey refers to Lacan's mirror stage.

The cinema, she says, similarly produces "structures of fascination [that are] strong enough to allow temporary loss of ego while simultaneously reinforcing it" (*Feminist Film Theory* 62). In other words, the viewer is afforded a certain amount of pleasure by both recognizing and misrecognizing himself within the film's elements.

Mulvey deliberately characterizes the viewer as exclusively male. This is partly because film is considered an extension of patriarchal ideology, but also because of women's structural function within film's discursive configuration. In accord with film's inclination for visual pleasure, woman predominantly appears "coded for strong visual and erotic impact" (*Feminist Film Theory* 62). As such, women are overwhelmingly depicted as a kind of spectacle, valued only as a form of sexual display that is erotically charged in the service of hetero-normative desire. Woman, in this respect, is equated with **to-be-looked-at-ness**, so much so that she often generates a visual pleasure that runs counter to the flow of narrative. But it is also in this way that women are disproportionately portrayed as passive objects within narrative cinema while men serve as active protagonists. This dynamic further accounts for what Mulvey terms the **male gaze**. Woman's appearance as an object of visual display sets up the male protagonist as the one who looks. He is the "bearer of the look," which entails additional power in the sense that he serves as a point of identification for the viewer. "As the spectator identifies with the main male protagonist, he projects his look onto that of his like, his screen surrogate, so that the power of the male protagonist as he controls events coincides with the active power of the erotic look, both giving a satisfying sense of omnipotence" (*Feminist Film Theory* 64). This is the point at which voyeurism comes together with film's narcissistic appeal. The viewer takes pleasure in viewing woman as a passive or erotic object while also being put in a position to identify with the protagonist who maintains greater discursive agency. Moreover, this relationship is part of the structural linchpin of dominant cinema. It allows the cinematic apparatus to deny its role in perpetuating the sexist ideologies of a patriarchal society.

In terms of appropriating psychoanalysis, Mulvey goes beyond the discursively structured gender relations within cinema to confront the paradox of phallocentrism or, rather, the way that woman's lack "produces the phallus as a symbolic presence" (*Feminist Film*

Theory 59). In this regard, the pleasure of woman as an erotic spectacle always entails the threat of castration. She simultaneously evokes anxiety, then, in that "the meaning of woman is sexual difference, the visually ascertainable absence of the penis" (*Feminist Film Theory* 65). Johnston outlined a similar stance in her earlier account, claiming that women always represent an intrusion or threat to the narrative and that "she is a traumatic presence which must be negated" (*Feminist Film Theory* 35). For Mulvey, there are two main ways in which Hollywood attempts to contain this threat. The first involves **sadism**. As part of this tendency, female characters are punished in some capacity. This may entail explicit physical or psychological violence, but it can also be enacted through less direct discursive measures. For example, women are regularly devalued within the narrative simply by being reduced to stereotypical or peripheral roles. The second way in which Hollywood attempts to suppress women's symbolic ties to castration is through **fetishism**.

In Freud's account, the fetish is a substitute object. It is something to which psychic energy is attached to **disavow** the anxiety associated with castration. In Mulvey's terms, fetishism refers more broadly to instances when film "builds up the physical beauty of the object, transforming it into something satisfying in itself" (*Feminist Film Theory* 65). She refers to the films of Josef von Sternberg in which the image is no longer contained by the male gaze. Instead, the image, in this instance of Marlene Dietrich, solicits a "direct erotic rapport with the spectator. The beauty of the woman as object and the screen space coalesce; she is no longer the bearer of guilt but a perfect product, whose body, stylized and fragmented by close-ups, is the content of the film and the direct recipient of the spectator's look" (*Feminist Film Theory* 65). In these moments, viewers are made aware of their own look, which implies something different than the typical exchange of looks Mulvey identifies as the crux of visual pleasure. This interpretation of fetishism also diverges from the more elaborate psychoanalytic explanations put forward by Freud and others. Partly for these reasons, fetishism remains a more problematic technique in Mulvey's account. Rather than contain the threat of castration, the fetishistic image, as Johnston observes, is "a projection of male narcissistic fantasy" and a "phallic replacement" which nonetheless acts as a symptom of its absence (*Feminist Film Theory* 34).

In this respect, Hollywood's efforts to contain sexual difference only serve to reproduce the paradox of phallocentrism.

Mulvey's essay provided feminist film theory with a watershed moment. It brought into clear focus feminists' primary objective and it outlined a method for appropriating existing theoretical discourse for this purpose. Although the essay distinguished Mulvey as a kind of singular force, many of her ideas were in concert with a much broader groundswell of feminist activity. In addition to the work of Johnston and others at *Screen*, Mulvey's essay corresponded with the emergence of several new journals specifically dedicated to feminist scholarship. These included *Women and Film, Camera Obscura, m/f, Differences*, and *Signs*. Another measure of Mulvey's success was the extensive response that she provoked. This included several points of criticism including a general questioning of psychoanalysis' suitability for feminism. Julia Lesage, for example, criticized *Screen*'s general acceptance of psychoanalytic theory in the strongest terms possible, arguing that its premises "are not only false but overtly sexist and as such demand political refutation."[12] B. Ruby Rich shares some of these reservations in her distinction between two different types of feminist activity. For her, there is an American-style of feminist criticism that is largely pragmatic and closely associated with ideas like "the personal is the political." By contrast, Rich classifies British feminists like Mulvey and Johnston as part of a more theoretical approach that she finds "unduly pessimistic."[13] Similar descriptions were applied to a number of French feminists (e.g. Julia Kristeva, Luce Irigaray, Hélène Cixous, and Monique Wittig). Though these theorists were just as important to the overall ferment of feminist scholarship at this time, some critics remained wary of their commitment to psychoanalysis and their willingness to adopt various post-structuralist styles (including a version of *écriture féminine*).

To a certain extent, Mulvey was fully aware that feminist theory required a practical component. In fact, Mulvey's call for a total negation of the existing system of cinema was part of an effort to outline the parameters of an alternative practice or, more specifically, a feminist counter-cinema. In analyzing the ways that patriarchy structures unconscious desires, Mulvey highlights the importance of establishing a practice that does more than merely challenge social and material forms of oppression. Instead, evoking the French feminists, she calls for cinematic forms capable of conceiving "a new language of desire" (*Feminist Film Theory* 60). Mulvey pursued this direction herself in making *Riddles of the Sphinx* (1977) and several other films with Peter Wollen. The experimental style of these films paralleled the work of feminist filmmakers like Yvonne Rainer, Sally Potter, and Chantal Akerman as well as more established narrative filmmakers like Agnes Varda and Marguerite Duras. Whereas these filmmakers generally subscribed to the principles of political modernism, Johnston had something different in mind when she called for a women's counter-cinema. For her, it involved returning to and reclaiming female directors like Dorothy Arzner, Lois Weber, and Ida Lupino, as well as more recent figures like Maya Deren. In this case, counter-cinema was less of a call to action than a call to rethink women's contribution to cinema as a kind of counter-history. This was more than just an opportunity to celebrate the accomplishments of these directors; it was also a way to use their experience as a model for future efforts. In these different calls for a feminist counter-cinema, both Mulvey and Johnston suggest that theory is one component in a broader critical endeavor that includes practical and historical considerations.

In the same way that the appeal to counter-cinema echoed the developments taking place at *Screen*, there was another parallel in feminist film theorists' efforts to advance new methods of critical textual analysis. These efforts began with the return to the work of earlier female directors and a growing interest in the "women's film," a genre that like film noir was formed mainly by virtue of its critical reception.[14] In both cases, feminist critics employed the logic outlined in relation to Comolli and Narboni's conflicted fifth category of films. That is, feminist critics approached these films as evidence of the contradictions inherent within patriarchal ideology. This approach was welcomed because it provided considerable flexibility. However, for this same reason, it occasionally sparked intense debate.

One of the most vigorous exchanges among feminist critics, for example, came in response to *Stella Dallas* (1937). In E. Ann Kaplan's analysis, the mother–daughter relationship at the center of the film transgresses what is considered proper and must be "curtailed and subordinated to what patriarchy considers best for the child" (*Feminism and Film* 475). The film's final scene, moreover, in presenting Stella's gaze, conveys "what it is to be a Mother in patriarchy," forced "to renounce, to be on the outside, and to take pleasure in this positioning" (*Feminism and Film* 476). By contrast, **Linda Williams** suggests that the film offers conflicting viewpoints and that in this regard cannot be reduced to merely a patriarchal containment of motherhood. Instead, as a film that "both addresses female audiences and contains important structures of viewing between women," *Stella Dallas* suggests "that it does not take a radical and consciously feminist break with patriarchal ideology to represent the contradictory aspects of the woman's position under patriarchy" (*Feminism and Film* 498). As with previous debates, this type of exchange sometimes created an impasse in the short term. But debate also forced both sides to further clarify their logic and rethink their conclusions. This propelled further investigation and often helped to foster a more rigorous standard of scholarship.

In addition to the general concerns about the significance of psychoanalysis in "Visual Pleasure and Narrative Cinema," there were several issues in Mulvey's essay that, like *Stella Dallas*, generated more acute points of disagreement. One question concerned the male gaze and the assumption that the erotic spectacle targeted heterosexual male desire exclusively. Several subsequent feminist scholars were able to identify a diverse variety of counter-examples that indicated otherwise. Miriam Hansen, for example, examined the case of Rudolf Valentino, a conspicuously eroticized male star of the 1920s with an intense female following. In another counter-example, Maureen Turim pointed to the musical number in *Gentlemen Prefer Blondes* (1953) where Jane Russell's character is surrounded by group of ornamental Olympic male athletes engaged in choreographed exercise.[15] Other scholars like Tania Modleski found that films such as Alfred Hitchcock's *Vertigo* (1958) constituted a far more complicated example than Mulvey suggests in her brief reference to it.[16]

The other major question that followed Mulvey's essay concerned the female spectator and the possibility of reclaiming some form of pleasure within spectatorship. Whereas Mulvey specifically addresses the viewer as male, many commentators quickly criticized this premise as untenable. It was obvious that women also view Hollywood cinema. This recalled the distinction made by earlier theorists like Baudry and Metz between the spectator as a discursively constructed subject position and the audience member as an actual viewer. However, if Mulvey is correct and narrative cinema constructs a gender-specific subject position, she then suggests that there is a profound incongruity whereby a significant number of viewers are discursively compelled to take pleasure in their own subjugation. But if this is not the case, then the question remains of how to account for potential variations without resorting to rudimentary forms of ethnography (i.e., asking individual viewers about their experience). As a way around these problems, several scholars posited specific viewing strategies that were available to actual viewers. For example, Mulvey, as part of a reconsideration of her earlier account, allows for the possibility of a trans- or bi-sexual viewing position. In certain cases at least, according to this revision, identification need not be an immutable process or categorically determined by gender. Conversely, Mary Anne Doane introduced **masquerade** as another means of resisting patriarchal structures. This refers to instances in which women on screen embrace a kind of excessive femininity, fully acknowledging that this position is culturally constructed. This speaks to the fact that identification and other forms of psychical investment cannot be physically coerced. Viewers retain some degree of agency and this can be manifest either through direct forms of opposition or through a self-reflexive awareness of culture's prevailing conventions.

These reconsiderations and elaborations were part of feminist film theory's ongoing expansion that continued well into the 1980s and early 1990s. While some scholars moved beyond film to analyze other types of media and popular culture (e.g. romance novels, soap operas, and music videos), many feminist theorists continued to address the questions raised in Mulvey's account. One example of such scholarship is the work of ***Kaja Silverman***. Starting from a more fully developed Lacanian position established in her first book, *The Subject of Semiotics*, Silverman begins with the premise that "there is a castration which precedes the recognition of anatomical difference—a castration to which all cultural subjects must submit" (*Acoustic Mirror* 1). She then takes cinema to be a system of representation that works in concert with the dominant ideology to conceal this condition. Psychoanalysis provides an interpretive method that allows her to diagnose the incongruities and contradictions that are manifest as part of this system. In accordance with Mulvey's general thesis, Silverman contends that male characters are provided with an appearance of unity and wholeness while anatomical deficiency is projected onto female characters through a series of discursive measures. This follows the related premise that gender is socially constructed, but is more forceful in showing the role of discourse in establishing and then reinforcing a cultural hierarchy between different sexes.

In *The Acoustic Mirror*, Silverman elaborates this argument by analyzing how Hollywood's use of sound is analogous to the operation of suture. This means that sound, both as a discursive and narrative device, works to cover over the male subject's symbolic castration. As in MacCabe's reference to *American Graffiti*, this is most often evident in the way that male characters are afforded a privileged relationship to synchronization (i.e., the way that sound and image are made to correspond). To illustrate, Silverman further considers *Singin' in the Rain* (1952) one of Hollywood's most celebrated accounts of its own assimilation of sound technologies. In the film's narrative, male characters negotiate this transition without incident. In contrast, the fictional studio's female star, Lina Lamont (Jean Hagen), suffers a series of humiliations because her voice does not match her otherwise glamorous outward appearance. According to Silverman, these humiliations tend to play out in spatial terms and Hollywood, more generally, tends to associate female characters with interiority while male characters are associated with exteriority. In this regard, "'Inside' comes to designate a recessed space within the story, while 'outside' refers to those elements of the story which seem in one way or another to frame that recessed space. Woman is confined to the former, and man to the latter" (*Acoustic Mirror* 54). Although Silverman goes on to consider the ways in which feminist filmmakers use the sound–image relationship to different ends, her analysis reinforces Mulvey's general critique that dominant cinema is structured in a way that supports patriarchal ideology.

While much of Silverman's work remained in fundamental agreement with Mulvey, she also contributed to important new developments like the increased interest in **masochism**. Early on, commentators like D. N. Rodowick raised questions about Mulvey's strict binary logic in terms of categorizing males as active and females as passive.[17] According to this logic, Hollywood is considered patriarchal precisely because of its sadistic subjugation of women. Most were willing to concur that Hollywood participated in this tradition; however, this assumption tended to downplay the possibility of other types of pleasure, especially perverse forms of desire that fell outside of accepted norms. In the book that followed *The Acoustic Mirror*, Silverman more fully explored this possibility in terms of several examples that explicitly dramatize the vulnerability of masculinity and that are tied to moments of historical **trauma**.[18] She considers, for instance, the male subject position within Hollywood films like *It's A Wonderful Life* (1946) and *The Best Years of Our Lives* (1946), as well as several films by the German director Rainer Werner Fassbinder.

As an extension of this interest, several feminist film scholars were drawn to the horror genre. This was somewhat counter-intuitive in that horror seemed to typify all of the worst assumptions enumerated by Mulvey. It appeared to be the genre that was most clearly organized around a sadistic, controlling camera focused on a passive, female victim. In Carol Clover's analysis, however, these assumptions quickly become problematic. In the slasher sub-genre, for example, many films featured impotent killers who resort to violence as compensation for their sexual deficiencies. Female characters, by contrast, not only withstand their violent attacks but also fight back and eventually prevail. Clover, similar to Rodowick's earlier analysis, suggests that the horror genre draws special attention to a masochistic position. She indicates that this position is figured as painful and feminine, but that it solicits male viewers. In her final analysis, horror films are adamant in suggesting that film's pleasure cannot be reduced to sadism. Although "the female body [still] structures the male drama," Clover suggests that pleasure, identification, and the formal relationships associated with looking are much more complicated than Mulvey implies (*Men, Women, and Chainsaws* 218).

Linda Williams' study of pornography represents another interesting development. As a genre, pornography, like horror, is seen as epitomizing patriarchy. And, more generally, it is considered devoid of any kind of cultural or intellectual value. Williams, however, yields several important insights through a series of close readings that combine historical and theoretical analysis. For instance,

Williams draws attention to the function of the so-called money shot within pornographic films. In her analysis, the climatic scene of male ejaculation demonstrates the genre's insistence on framing sexual pleasure in strictly phallic terms. This is another example of fetishistic disavowal or, rather, "a solution offered by hard-core film to the perennial male problem of understanding woman's difference." Although Williams shows that this solution is fundamentally problematic, she also maintains that understanding its contradictions can lead to new ways of resisting phallocentrism (*Hardcore* 119). This hearkens back to Mulvey's call for a new language of desire and what other feminists labeled *jouissance*, a type of pleasure that exists outside of patriarchal hegemony. At the same time, the work of Williams, Clover, and Silverman illustrates a general divide between feminist theorists dedicated to a scholarly analysis of patriarchy and those who were committed to enacting feminist principles through new forms of social and aesthetic expression.

As part of his overall assessment of this period, Rodowick concludes that "the lessons of feminist theory and criticism have in fact set the standard [. . .] for the role of oppositional intellectuals in their challenge to the norms of knowledge and power in the reigning discursive formations" (*Crisis of Political Modernism* 294). This accomplishment encompassed a wide range of critical strategies and many more individual theorists than have been mentioned here. On the whole, however, feminist film theory provided a basis for deconstructing the dominant ideology in general and patriarchy more specifically, in effect accelerating and further focusing the work that was already underway at *Screen* and throughout the emerging field of film study. For Teresa de Lauretis, the most important part of this overall development was that feminist theory produced "a new social subject, women: as speakers, writers, readers, spectators, users and makers of cultural forms, shapers of cultural processes" ("Aesthetic and Feminist Theory" 163). Women marked a new subject position or modality precisely in the sense that prior to feminists' intervention they had been barred by social constraints from many cultural practices and, more specifically, the institutional sites where knowledge is produced. In terms of bringing this new position into being, feminist theory established an important model for others who were likewise constrained by socially constructed manifestations of difference.

In this regard, it helped to advance the important work that followed in relation to questions of race, ethnicity, and sexuality, but in doing so it was also forced to confront the challenge of how these new positions related to one another.

POST-COLONIAL THEORY

Post-colonial theory, similar to feminist film theory, begins outside the scope of film study and involves a much broader array of influences and concerns. It took shape in the aftermath of World War II in response to the realities of decolonization and as part of the ongoing struggles undertaken by peoples of color across the globe. It encompasses the social and political efforts to overcome colonial rule and its legacies, as well as the critical and theoretical interrogation of Euro-centrism. In this regard, post-colonial theory often intersects with the struggles of racial and ethnic minorities, diasporic communities, and indigenous groups, and it is equally valuable in understanding their fight against racism, discrimination, and hegemonic power. In Ella Shohat and Robert Stam's magisterial account, *Unthinking Eurocentrism*, post-colonial theory is further extended to later developments like multiculturalism and globalization. With respect to film, the significance of post-colonial theory, much like feminist film theory, is clearest in its ties to a specific form of counter-cinema, its introduction of different theoretical influences, and in the new methods of critical analysis it facilitated.

In the late 1960s, filmmakers and activists outside of the industrialized West began calling for a counter-cinema that specifically addressed the history and effects of colonialism. This call was articulated in a series of manifestos, most famously Fernando Solanas and Octavio Getino's "Towards a **Third Cinema**," and was initially associated with Latin American movements like Brazil's Cinema Novo and post-revolutionary Cuban filmmakers like Tomás Gutiérrez Alea. In these various declarations, Third Cinema is defined in opposition to First World systems of commercial production like Hollywood as well as other established practices like European art cinema and state-sponsored national cinemas. More generally, it is characterized as part of a militant rejection of capitalist imperialism and bourgeois society.

In some respects, Third Cinema resembled the counter-cinemas advocated at *Screen* and by feminist film theorists. There were certainly several common points of reference. Solanas and Getino, for instance, mention the influence of European filmmakers like Jean Luc Godard and Chris Marker. They and many of their associates also adopted the Marxist aesthetic practices devised by Bertolt Brecht. At the same time, these theorists and practitioners were wary of Western intellectuals and their ties to Euro-centric traditions. Part of the purpose of calling for a Third Cinema was to combat the effects of cultural imperialism and the way in which cinematic representations reproduce discriminatory practices in the aftermath of colonial rule. To this end, a key distinction with European counter-cinemas was that even while Third Cinema endorsed formal experimentation, it also insisted on an awareness of the historical conditions that structured the colonial situation. In its effort to redress these conditions, Third Cinema also recognized the importance of adaptation and flexibility, stressing the need for pragmatism to have its desired effect. This also means that different groups were shaped by very different historical influences or political circumstances. For instance, some Latin American groups were influenced by Italian neorealism and the documentary tradition established by John Grierson. French filmmaker, Jean Rouch, was by contrast the most prominent influence for many post-colonial African filmmakers. As a result of these variations, it is difficult to precisely identify its theoretical principles.

As part of its antagonism with the West and Euro-centrism, post-colonial theorists turned to new theoretical influences to fortify and expand the calls for a Third Cinema practice. Whereas the scholars associated with *Screen* and feminism primarily relied on the developments in France discussed in Chapter 2, Third World film theorists found inspiration in the work of subversive intellectuals like Frantz Fanon. Fanon was important in at least two different ways. First, the polemical rhetoric in *The Wretched of the Earth* reinforced the revolutionary undercurrents that were growing among political activists and dissidents. Second, his work in *Black Skin White Mask* examines how racial difference is marked in a visual exchange related to the colonial situation and how this exchange has a residual impact on black consciousness. As in de Beauvoir's account of woman as Other, Fanon's analysis of the psychological dimensions of colonial power relations delineates otherness as a socially manifest basis for subjugation.

Edward Said's account of **Orientalism** provided a related theoretical touchstone. He shows that this term, a designation historically applied to Asia and the Middle East, is largely constructed from the perspective of the West. This indicates another case in which the Other is socially and discursively constructed. As in feminist analyses of patriarchal ideology, this supposition exposes a structural dependency between the two in which the negative attributes ascribed to the subordinate group serve to conceal the contradictions and inconsistencies that are the crux of the overarching system. Similar to psychoanalytic formulations of the self-other dynamic, difference structures identity, but it does so in a way that difference is subsequently displaced and systematically contained. Though Said's account is couched in more direct references to European theorists like Foucault and Gramsci, it still marked an important advance for post-colonial theorists. In fact, and again like feminist theorists, post-colonial theorists were willing to appropriate different intellectual traditions as a matter of political pragmatism and fluidly combined these influences into new hybrid models. In an important example of this intermingling, post-colonial theorists drew inspiration from Mikhail Bakhtin, a Russian Formalist whose contributions were largely overlooked until the 1960s. In particular, Bahktin's account of the **carnivalesque**, a cultural practice in which traditional hierarchies are inverted, provided an alternative model of pleasure and subversion.

The combination of these developments in turn prompted more critical forms of analysis. As a matter of applying these new theoretical influences and further elaborating the basis of a post-colonial counter-cinema, many film scholars began focusing their attention on analyzing specific textual and cultural examples of Euro-centrism and colonialist ideology. In the broadest sense possible, this perspective extended to questions about the politics of representation in general and the role of racial and ethnic minorities within dominant cinemas like Hollywood. These concerns were especially evident in the growing scrutiny devoted to the history of racist practices such as blackface and the problematic stereotypes they perpetuated. In Michael Rogin's analysis, for example, these practices were not just evidence of vulgar hatred or fear of the unknown but part of a deeper structural logic. In specific cases like *The Jazz Singer* (1927), he shows how one ethnic group is able to assimilate into the social majority by virtue of subjugating another group on the basis of racial difference. In another sense, the developments associated with post-colonial theory coincided with an effort to question the limitations and oversights within film theory's initial formation. For instance, bell hooks specifically questions the inability of Mulvey and other feminists to address black female spectators. In her analysis, this position necessitates an oppositional practice. That is, by both refusing to identify with white female characters and the phallocentric gaze, black female spectators continually deconstruct the binary logic implicit in Mulvey's argument.[19]

In the same way that hooks, as part of her analysis, acknowledges the need to identify the positive attributes associated with the black female viewing position, **Homi Bhabha** suggests that post-colonial theory does not need to be entirely limited to the history of domination and oppression. To this end, he explores the potential within cultural difference and the interstitial or liminal spaces that it facilitates. He writes, for instance, that the "interstitial passage between fixed identifications opens up the possibility of a cultural hybridity that entertains difference without an assumed or imposed hierarchy" (*Location of Culture* 4). In other words, Bhabha sees the post-colonial subject, who wavers somewhere in between indigenous and colonial cultures, as an opportunity to move beyond and escape existing concepts. This type of ambivalence, as in the spectator position detailed by hooks, poses the possibility of breaking down binary logic and creating something new that cannot be reduced to an absolute or totalized meaning. To further illustrate this possibility, Bhabha reconsiders the function of stereotypes. Similar to feminists' strategic use of masquerade, he contends that stereotypes do more to expose the contradictions and fragility of racial domination.

Bhabha's willingness to embrace the fluidity of the post-colonial subject and the hybridity of post-colonial theory more generally is also evident in the work of theorist and filmmaker **Trinh T. Minh-Ha**. For Trinh, as with many of the feminist film theorists introduced in the previous section and the queer theorists that will be addressed in the following section, this approach is part of a larger interest in post-structuralist critique. Whereas there is a tendency among some of these scholars to simply celebrate the dissolution of existing structures, others like Trinh take it to be a more fundamental measure and necessary reproach to the continued entrenchment of patriarchy, capitalism, Euro-centrism, and other systems of domination. According to this view, the figurative master(s) "may allow us temporarily to beat him at his own game, but they will never enable us to bring about genuine change" (*Woman, Native, Other* 80). As an extension of her critique, Trinh questions the role of the academy in assimilating the subversive and counter-hegemonic elements in feminist and post-colonial thought. To illustrate this, she recounts the difficulty she had in publishing the theoretical text, *Woman, Native, Other.*

> For academics, "scholarly" is a normative territory that they own all for themselves, hence theory is no theory if it is not dispensed in a way recognizable to and validated by them. The mixing of different modes of writing; the mutual challenge of theoretical and poetical, discursive and "non-discursive" languages; the strategic use of stereotyped expressions in exposing stereotypical thinking; all these attempts at introducing a break into the fixed norms of the Master's confident prevailing discourses are easily misread, dismissed, or obscured in the name of "good writing," or "theory," or of "scholarly work."
>
> (*Framer Framed* 138)

Trinh explores these intersections between theory and poetry not only in her writing but also in her filmmaking practice. Her films *Reassemblage* (1982) and *Surname Viet Given Name Nam* (1989) both challenge conventional notions about knowledge and representation by combining elements of documentary and ethnography with modernist techniques. Subsequent critics have labeled these works experimental or hybrid. **Bill Nichols**, film study's leading theorist of documentary, describes this style of documentary as performative. It goes beyond the reflexivity and intertextuality of previous counter-cinemas while still blurring the discursive boundaries between knowledge and action. What further distinguishes this mode is its emphasis on embodied knowledge (e.g. memory, affect, and subjective experience) and stylized expressivity, "while also retaining a referential claim to the historical" (*Blurred Boundaries* 98).

As part of this performative style, Trinh uses contentious strat-egies like reenactment. Many disapprove of this device since it appears deceitful and can be misleading, especially in the context of documentary. In *Surname Viet Given Name Nam*, for example, women within the film recite what appears to be autobiographical testimony but that is in fact not theirs. Trinh explains this strategy in terms of voice and in a way that explicitly recalls Gayatry Spivak's question, "Can the subaltern speak?" As Trinh puts it, "I can't say here that I only wanted to empower women, or as people like to put it, to 'give voice' to the women involved. The notion of giving voice is so charged because you have to be in such a position that you can 'give voice' to other people." Similar to the way that Spivak uses her question to critique the propensity of Western intellectu-als to claim to know the discourse of society's Other, Trinh claims that "the notion of giving voice remains extremely paternalistic" (*Framer Framed* 169). At the same time, she does not reject this idea entirely but rather hints at a different notion of voice. In describing the women who speak in the film, Trinh says that they "are asked both to embody other selves, other voices, and to drift back to their own selves, which are not really their 'natural' selves but the selves they want to present" (*Framer Framed* 146). They speak, then, with a voice that is at once theirs and not theirs and with a plurality that both exceeds and undermines notions of individual agency. This, in turn, speaks to the complicated history of colonialism and the simul-taneity of multiple cultures grafted onto a single body.

Similar to feminist film theory, post-colonial theory introduced a series of new subject positions that called attention both to those who had been previously excluded and the issues that demanded urgent attention following the formation of these new modalities. As with the other developments discussed in this chapter, post-colonial theorists were committed to a number of different critical endeavors. On one hand, they were involved in articulating a post-colonial counter-cinema that specifically addressed the social and aesthetic interests of those outside of the West and others engaged in political struggles against colonialist ideology. On the other hand, post-colonial theory involved locating new theoretical influences and developing new methods of critical analysis, drawing particular attention to the history of racism and related forms of structural domination. While these different directions divided post-colonial theory into a wide variety of competing agendas, some theorists like Trinh were able to maintain a productive middle ground between theory and practice. More broadly, post-colonial theory represents a more diffuse critical framework. It extends well beyond the scope of film and visual representation and is concerned with larger questions about culture, politics, and global relations.

QUEER THEORY

Queer theory marks another important development within and alongside film theory. As with the theoretical formations covered in the two previous sections, queer theory grew out of a larger gay liberation movement and through a series of protest efforts that confronted the harassment and discriminatory practices sanctioned as part of hetero-normative society. These efforts began in the 1950s and gained momentum among the social upheavals and flourishing counter-cultures of the 1960s. They gained additional focus in the 1980s as groups like ACT-UP confronted the growing AIDS crisis and responded to attacks by culturally conservative groups. These efforts came together with the term "queer," an appropriation of a one-time pejorative that indicates the emergence of a social and political consciousness among gay, lesbian, bi-sexual, and trans-gender individuals. In this regard, sexuality and sexual identity, like gender, race, and ethnicity, are considered socially constructed distinctions. These distinctions both constitute difference and serve as a basis for structuring or maintaining the cultural norms. Queer theory provides a critical framework for analyzing these operations as they pertain to the dominant ideology. With respect to film, it draws further attention to the way in which visual representations perpetuate homophobic stereotypes and reinforce existing power dynamics. At the same time, queer theory recognizes queerness as a site of transgression and as an opportunity to resist or subvert normative social relations.

In many ways, queer theory emerged as a continuation of the initial response to Mulvey's "Visual Pleasure and Narrative Cinema." Like other feminist scholars, queer theorists questioned Mulvey's rigid, and largely hetero-normative, conceptions of identity and pleasure. These concerns focused primarily on the question of lesbian desire. This was followed by a reassessment of the relationships between female characters within Hollywood cinema and renewed debates about the female gaze. According to Mulvey's formulation, visual pleasure is structured around the erotic display of women. As such, the gaze appears compatible with lesbian desire. However, this also suggests an uneasy alignment between lesbian desire and the patriarchal male gaze. These dilemmas raised larger questions about the merit of psychoanalytic theory. In some cases, debate went so far as to suggest that there are irreconcilable differences between feminists and queer theorists.

Feminist scholars like **Teresa de Lauretis**, who also played a prominent role in pioneering queer theory, advocated a return to, rather than the rejection of, psychoanalysis. These efforts yielded an increasingly sophisticated understanding of the complex history of psychoanalysis and its conceptual nuances. For instance, de Lauretis examines the significance of **fantasy** as a concept that problematizes strict binary distinctions between male and female subject positions and the relationship between socially prescribed psychic structures like the oedipal complex and unconscious desire more generally.[20] This type of critical re-engagement with psychoanalysis is similarly evident in the work of scholars like Judith Mayne, Patricia White, Leo Bersani, and Lee Edelman, among many others.

Despite the insights produced as part of this scholarship, the return to psychoanalysis was also fraught with challenges. In de Lauretis' view, for example, it is necessary to re-read Freud from a perspective of "sexual (in)difference," a formulation that demonstrates "the discursive double bind" within which she claims lesbianism is caught (*Practice of Love* 4). This perspective thus marks the need to renegotiate both orthodox and feminist interpretations of Freudian psychoanalysis. Another complication in this return concerns its relationship to post-structuralism and French feminism. As an extension of sexual (in)difference, de Lauretis adopts Monique Wittig's "linguistically impossible subject pronoun": "j/e." As another discursive intervention, it shows that lesbian representation "is not and cannot be a reappropriation of the female body as it is, domesticated, maternal, oedipally or preoedipally en-gendered, but is a struggle to transcend both gender and 'sex' and re-create the body other-wise: to see it perhaps as monstrous, or grotesque, or mortal, or violent, and certainly also sexual, but with a material and sensual specificity that will resist phallic idealization and render it accessible to women in another sociosexual economy" (*Feminism and Film* 394). This strategy recalls post-colonial theorists like Trinh who is likewise conscious of the need to create new ways of thinking that cannot be reclaimed by existing structures of knowledge. However, in terms of framing this new position as having a distinct specificity, there is some suggestion that there is an innate feminine or lesbian essence that requires its own unique form of language. Along with concerns that this type of strategy, and *écriture féminine* more generally, slipped into an unwitting form of essentialism, there were also questions as to whether this approach took queer theory too far afield from its social and political objectives.

Although her work is largely set outside of film studies, the most significant contemporary queer theorist is **Judith Butler**. Similar to de Lauretis, Butler's work both returns to and critically questions the influence of psychoanalysis and its French interlocutors. Her work stands out, however, in the way that she takes the anti-essentialist position advocated by many feminists to its logical conclusion. In this regard, Butler argues not only that gender is constructed as part of a hetero-normative system, but also that sex, as a biological category, is likewise contrived as a matter of discourse. Both sex and gender in this view are products of a regulatory regime that determines legibility or, rather, what is made to appear as difference. These categories, as a result, do not exist in their own right but are manifest through the "repeated stylization of the body [and the] set of repeated acts within a highly rigid regulatory frame that congeal over time to produce the appearance of substance, of a natural sort of being" (*Gender Trouble* 43–4).

Butler further denaturalizes gender by defining it in terms of performativity, a notion drawn from J. L. Austin's account of speech acts and the particular formulations in which meaning is enacted as a condition of enunciation (e.g. the statement "I do" in the context of a wedding or a baseball umpire declaring "you're out"). This means that gender does not exist at an ontological level. Instead, it "is performatively constituted by the very 'expressions' that are said to be its results" (*Gender Trouble* 33). According to this assessment, it is no longer necessary for queer theorists to construct a new sub-ject position or representational parameters. On the contrary, queer identities highlight the constructed status of sexual difference and the inherent instability of that construction. In other words, they decon-struct and displace the possibility of sexuality as "a naturalistic neces-sity" (*Gender Trouble* 44). In reconstructing this construction, queer subjects effectively perform a parody of the existing social-sexual regime. Butler thus transvalues the deviancy that has always trou-bled gender normativity and imbues it with a potential for political agency.

Although Butler's 1990 book *Gender Trouble* is best known as a major landmark in the emergence of queer theory as an important new area of scholarly inquiry, it did raise several key questions with regard to representation. This was particularly clear in her later anal-ysis of *Paris Is Burning* (1990), a documentary about the drag queen subcutlure in New York. This interest in cross-dressing as a form of gender masquerade more broadly intersects with the interpretive strategy known as **camp**. For Susan Sontag, camp primarily refers to a sensibility that emphasizes artifice and exaggeration. However, she goes on to note an extensive array of associations including several styles and figures, many of which had links to popular culture and entertainment. For instance, Hollywood stars ranging from Greta Garbo and Bette Davis to Mae West and Jayne Mansfield are consid-ered camp or campy. Sontag also indicates that it functions as a pri-vate code. In this sense, camp is like the term queer, meaning both a recognition of something within a film that stands out as ostentatious but also something that is out of place or uncanny. It is also in this sense that camp is more than a descriptive term.

Camp is something that queer audiences employ as part of a **decoding** practice also referred to as queering that either embel-lishes or foregrounds certain textual elements. This allows a film like *The Wizard of Oz* (1939), with its theme of escape to a fabulous fantasy world, to be read as having a queer sub-text. This practice can also be used in a more active sense to highlight unintentional elements, for instance the tacit homoerotic undertones between two male stars. These practices, like the drag queens that Butler analyzes in *Paris Is Burning*, combine defiance with affirmation. They also outline the possibility of creating new communities around a model of reception that is at once more advanced in discerning connotative meanings and aware of a utopian quality that exceeds film's semiotic dimensions. For Richard Dyer, the musical is particularly adept at producing the type of emotional or affective intensities that can reconcile the inadequacies of lived reality with the possibility of an imaginary solution. Although this utopian aspect of popular entertainment is not articulated in direct relationship to queer theory, it resonates with the ability of gay audiences to formulate a productive mode of spectatorship despite Hollywood's relentlessly heterosexual orientation.

In addition to the developments associated with theorists like de Lauretis and Butler and the emergence of camp, queer theory, much like the other theoretical sub-fields taking shape during this period, encompassed several related critical efforts. This included the rediscovery of early queer films like *Maedchen in Uniform* (1931) and the reclaiming of early figures like Dorothy Arzner as not only a feminist but also queer. Queer theory also involved developing methods of critical analysis based on Hollywood's initial efforts to address gay characters and themes in films like *Personal Best* (1982) and *Cruising* (1980). In terms of the post-war period, queer theorists helped to identify the different histories and influences that make up queer cinema. In the US, for example, queer cinema has roots in the work of 1950s and 1960s avant-garde and underground filmmakers like Kenneth Anger, Jack Smith, and Andy Warhol. Several directors working in the tradition of European art cinema have also been important contributors. In addition to Fassbinder and Pasolini, this list includes Derek Jarman, Pedro Almodovar, and Ulrike Ottinger. By the 1990s, a new queer cinema began to take shape featuring the work of independent directors like Gus Van Sant and Todd Haynes as well as more alternative filmmakers ranging from John Waters to Su Friedrich and Sadie Benning. Documentaries like *The Celluloid Closet* (1995) and *Before Stonewall* (1984) brought the LGBT community further into the spotlight. The more recent success of films like *Boys Don't Cry* (1999), *Hedwig and the Angry Inch* (2001), *Brokeback Mountain* (2005), and *Harvey Milk* (2008) has continued this progress.

The mainstream success of these films has in some ways rendered the issues raised by queer theorists more visible than many of the concerns confronted by feminists and post-colonial theorists. Yet it is clear that numerous challenges remain. In this regard, Marlon Riggs' *Tongues Untied* (1989) is an important representative of the complexities that continue to preoccupy queer theorists today. Though highly regarded by critics, the film became a lightning rod with conservative politicians because part of its funding had come from public sources. This reaction was consistent with a more general backlash against identity politics and many of the other social issues that had inspired important theoretical work undertaken as part of Screen Theory.

As a film, *Tongues Untied* resembles Trinh's stylistic and thematic interests. For example, it is also described as a performative documentary with an emphasis on embodied knowledge. And with its focus on the doubly silenced group of black gay men, it is likewise concerned with finding a voice. To this end, the film creates a collage of different sounds and voices. At times, this results in an unnerving cacophony. At other times these elements are synchronized to produce harmonic rhythms. For Kobena Mercer, in his analysis of the film together with Isaac Julien's *Looking for Langston* (1989), this type of "dialogic voicing" is necessary to account for the multidimensionality incumbent within any collective identity.[21] The film takes this further with its conclusion. After Riggs proclaims that he is no longer mute, the film ends with an illustrated but soundless "Snap!" The term echoes an earlier scene in which a number of drag queens and snap divas provide a tongue-in-cheek crash course in the coded non-verbal language of snapping. In refusing to synchronize sound and image here, the film suggests both defiance and affirmation. Much of the film affirms difference while also dislocating it. Again, in its final gesture, *Tongues Untied* affirms the power of voice but only to dislocate it—linking it to the past, to others, and to the possibility of something else.

A POST-MODERN END

In the 1980s and early 1990s, the term **post–modern** gained prominence as both an emerging sensibility and a new theoretical distinction. In many ways, this new focus was a continuation and expansion of several post-1968 intellectual developments. It was also another area heavily influenced by French theory. French philosopher Jean-Francois Lyotard, for example, provided one of the first definitions of what he termed the post-modern condition. Specifically, he associates post-modernity with the loss of meta-narratives. Throughout the modern era, systems of knowledge have been supported or legitimized by various "grand" narratives ranging from religious notions of a divine creator to Marx's account of historical progress. For Lyotard, these narratives begin to dissipate at an accelerated rate in the second half of the twentieth century.

In many respects, the work of theorists discussed in this chapter contributed to this process. Following the general advances of post-structuralism, feminists, post-colonial theorists, and queer theorists directly questioned existing systems of knowledge by deconstructing the hegemony of patriarchy, Euro-centrism, and heterosexual norms respectively and by advocating new systems based on multiplicity and pluralism. At the same time, however, post-modernity is closely linked to a shifting sensibility within consumer society. Jean Baudrillard, for instance, associated it primarily with the proliferation of simulations and a growing fetishization for what he and others classified as the hyperreal. In this case, post-modern refers to the growing indeterminacy between real and unreal, something Baudrillard further identifies, in a departure from structuralist semiotics, as signs that lack a stable referent. This development was forcefully illustrated through examples ranging from Disneyland to the predilection for illusory facades in the architecture of Las Vegas. In this regard, post-modern theory also marked a shift away from specific objects like film to more general considerations of culture, media, and art.

One of the most important theorists associated with post-modernity is *Fredric Jameson*. His work followed this general trajectory in that he adopted the term as he moved away from literature to a broader analysis of shifting stylistic patterns across culture. As part of his analysis, he identified key tropes like nostalgia, irony, and parody, and he draws a distinction in the way they function in different historical periods. As an example of modernist painting, Jameson suggests that Edvard Munch's *The Scream* parodies the dynamic between subjective feelings of alienation and their outward expression. By contrast, he later cites Brian De Palma's *Blow-Out* (1973) as an example of post-modernist cinema. *Blow-Out*, like Munch's painting, is about the construction of a scream, but for Jameson it lacks the same critical dimension. It is no longer a parody, but instead a form of pastiche or blank irony. In addition to the film's reference to Michelangelo Antonioni's *Blow-Up* (1966), *Blow-Out* simultaneously evokes the sound–image dynamics demonstrated in *American Graffiti* and *Singin' in the Rain*. It mocks the techniques evident in those films, but this gesture is entirely empty, neither negating its predecessors nor offering an actual alternative to them. In this case, post-modernism suggests a de-politicization of the techniques used by Trinh, Riggs, and those that served as a cornerstone for many of the counter-cinemas discussed throughout this chapter.

Whereas some theorists embraced the overall instability that flourished as part of post-modernity, Jameson, as a Marxist, maintained a more critical outlook. This is clearest in his description of post-modernity as the cultural logic of late-capitalism. Post-modernity, in this view, is not a way to escape history, but a way to attend to it. The shift in certain stylistic preferences, for example from parody to pastiche, is merely a cultural expression of changes taking place in the governing economic system. Cultural analysis, as a result, requires a diagnostic interpretation of these symptomatic manifestations or the recognition of an allegorical dimension as part of this relationship. As a kind of structuring absence, then, history is only evident by ascertaining what Jameson in an earlier work identified as the text's political unconscious.

In casting post-modernity as a historical development, Jameson's approach highlights several concurrent circumstances that were also influential as film theory concluded its formative period. First, the early 1990s marked the end of the Cold War. As several repressive governments collapsed and diplomatic relations between the East and West were renewed, there was much to celebrate. At the same time, this period echoed the aftermath of World War II. For all of its optimism, there was also a certain amount of consternation, especially as global capitalism took root throughout the former Eastern Bloc. These developments coincided with the growing emphasis on neoliberal economic principles in Anglo-American countries. Although the general public—following the social protest movements of the 1960s and the gradual success of new critical frameworks like film theory and feminism—often viewed the academy as a bastion of leftwing radicalism, neoliberal principles were also becoming more pronounced throughout the institutional organization of the university system. To some extent, these two developments were interrelated. In the US, the Cold War had played a significant role in supporting the expansion of higher education. The government subsidized tuition and allocated long-term grants. Though these policies were devoted primarily to improving science and technology, they also helped to enhance ancillary resources like university presses and indirectly helped other departments. As this funding began to decline in the 1980s, there was a greater emphasis on justifying the university in terms of neoliberal market principles.

By the end of the 1980s, film study was firmly established within the Anglo-American academy thanks in part to the intellectual richness and wide-ranging success of Screen Theory. But with shifting geopolitical and institutional dynamics on the horizon, there was also a sense of ambivalence about this accomplishment. This is particularly apparent in the changes taking place at *Screen*. In 1989, SEFT, the organization that founded *Screen*, disbanded and the journal relocated to the University of Glasgow. Up to that point, it had maintained a degree of institutional autonomy and many of its contributors drew a distinction between the work they did at *Screen* and the requirements that came with being a professional academic. This distinction was integral in the rationale that allowed burgeoning film theorists, both at *Screen* and many of the other journals founded during the same period, to believe that politics, aesthetics, and theory could coalesce as part of one larger critical project. By the mid-1990s, the academy was one of the last remaining venues for continuing the theoretical innovations of the previous two decades. By this time, talk of effecting social change may have continued but the connection between theory and practice was far less palpable.

At the same time that film theory lost some of its political valence, it remained a target in ongoing debates about the politics of culture. These debates escalated in 1996, for example with the so-called Sokal Affair. This refers to an incident when a leading theoretical journal, *Social Text*, published an essay by Alan Sokal.

The author revealed that the essay had been a hoax—a specious argument about quantum gravity built on a pastiche of references to French theory and post-modernism. For critics of theory, this was proof not only of theory's warped relativism but also its failure to uphold rigorous standards as an academic practice. Despite all that film theory had accomplished in terms of synthesizing different theoretical influences, developing methods of critical analysis, and empowering new and neglected subject positions, it was once again immersed in a larger crisis of legitimacy. Unlike the informal debates that took place in the first half of the twentieth century, these debates played out in the pages of scholarly journals and at professional conferences. Despite these more formal settings, there were several exchanges that triggered animosity and discord. And whereas debate in the past had contributed to film theory's advance, the implications of the growing antipathy toward theory after 1996 are less clear.

SUMMARY

In the 1970s and 1980s, film theory enjoyed a period of tremendous growth and development. It became closely associated with the British journal *Screen* where theorists adopted key components from French theory as the basis for critically analyzing film. Theoretical work stressed the ideological implications of dominant cinema as well as the need to develop principles for a counter-cinema and other counter-hegemonic practices. Feminist film theory became an especially important focal point during this time, synthesizing *Screen*'s theoretical interests with a more focused sense of political urgency. This served as a model for the subsequent emergence of post-colonial and queer theory, and for more general concerns about the relationship between identity and representation. As part of its success, film theory became more diffuse in addressing a wider array of interests and fostering debate about methodological priorities. As film theory moved into the academy, some of these debates escalated into larger questions about theory's purpose and its scholarly merits.

Questions

1. How does cinema reinforce the dominant ideology? What are the most important theoretical tools for analyzing cinema's ideological function?

2. Why do so many theorists stress the importance of developing a counter-cinema? What are some examples of counter-cinema and how does it engage viewers differently?

3. Why do theorists draw attention to how specific groups are represented on film? How do viewers relate to these representations? How do some viewers challenge these images?

4. Why did Laura Mulvey's essay, "Visual Pleasure and Narrative Cinema," have such an immense impact? What were some of the specific debates that followed it?

5. There are several brief references in this chapter to issues of sound and voice. If film is an audio-visual medium, why is sound so often overlooked? How does sound relate to the theoretical issues that developed during this period?

NOTES

1 Quoted in Bolas (2009): 12.
2 "Editorial." *Screen*, Vol. 10, No. 1 (January 1969): 3.
3 "Editorial." *Screen*, Vol. 12, No. 1 (Spring 1971): 5.
4 Ibid.
5 See *Screen*, Vol. 12, No. 4 (Winter 1971), *Screen*, Vol. 14, No. 4 (Winter 1973), and *Screen*, Vol. 15, No. 2 (Summer 1974) respectively.
6 See *Screen*, Vol. 14, No. 1–2 (Spring/Summer 1973).
7 See Peirce (1991).
8 See Heath's discussion of suture in *Questions of Cinema* (1981), especially: 82–3.
9 See "Godard and Counter-Cinema: *Vent d'Est*" in Wollen (1982).
10 See Barthes (1974).
11 See Chapter 16 in Gitlin's *The Sixties* (1987).
12 See Lesage (1974).
13 See Rich's essay, "The Crisis of Naming in Feminist Film Criticism," in Thornham (1999).

14 See Altman (1999) and Doane (1987).
15 See Hansen (1991) and Turim (1985).
16 See Modleski (1988).
17 See Rodowick (1991).
18 See Silverman (1992)
19 See hooks (1992: 313).
20 See de Lauretis (1994), 123–48.
21 See Kobena Mercer's "Dark and Lovely Too: Black Gay Men in Independent
    Film" in Gever, Greyson, and Parmar (1993).

POST-THEORY, 1996–2015

By the end of the twentieth century, film theory had established itself as a distinct scholarly discourse. In the period detailed in Chapter 3, film theory gained formal recognition as film and media study were integrated into the Anglo-American university system, often as part of an inter-disciplinary expansion of the traditional humanities departments like literature. This institutional framework provided important support in the discipline's advancement, facilitating access to additional resources (e.g. libraries, archives, screening venues, research assistance, etc.) and encouraging the field to develop more diligent professional standards. It also served to elevate the status of past developments like the debates initiated by early theorists and the influence of French theory. These steps were important in validating film theory's intellectual merit; they provided it with a sense of history and a series of methods, and, in turn, fostered a growing number of outlets for further investigation.

Despite film theory's overall success, the dilemmas associated with post-modernism in general and the Sokal Affair more specifically introduced a new crisis of legitimacy. This crisis no longer concerned the medium as such (as it had for film's earliest theorists) but, rather, the methods by which theory was carried out and the intellectual value of its objectives. Many of these concerns had been well documented throughout theory's ascent, but they became far more pronounced with David Bordwell and Noël Carroll's 1996 co-edited collection, *Post-Theory*. This book raised the profile of theory's critics and called into question many of the principles, especially those associated with French theory, that had dominated film theory for much of the past two decades. In addition to challenging these entrenched principles, theory's critics offered a series of alternative methods that promised to correct the excesses and fallacies that had precipitated the more recent crisis of legitimacy. *Post-Theory*, in this respect, marks an important intervention, but in framing theory and its critics as incompatible adversaries it also infused certain debates with an inordinate degree of vitriol.

While some critics called for an outright rejection of all film theory, *Post-Theory* was in another sense consistent with the broader shifts taking place as part of the discipline's changing institutional and intellectual status. As film and media studies were incorporated into the academy, theory in particular faced a kind of existential crisis. How would its anti-establishment politics, for instance, fit within the demands of academic standardization? How would the work of feminist, post-colonial, and queer theorists—specifically their analysis of power, difference, and identity along with their concurrent calls for counter-hegemonic forms of representation—be received amidst the corporatization of the university and mounting anti-intellectualism? To some extent, the angst prompted by these circumstances coincided with a growing affinity for introspection and re-evaluation within the discipline. In this regard, post-theory does not necessarily signal the end of theory. Instead, it largely means that as scholars have turned their attention inward to the discipline's formation and its various faults, theory no longer functions as a primary organizing principle, certainly not in the way it once did. This does not mean, however, that this scholarship is not theoretically informed or that it is without theoretical implications.

THEORY'S CRITICS, COGNITIVE SCIENCE, AND HISTORICAL POETICS

Film theorists have almost always embraced a critical perspective and a willingness to question existing assumptions about film and culture. The earliest film theorists, for instance, went against the belief that film did not warrant serious consideration. Realist film theorists like André Bazin went on to develop a position that challenged earlier formalist principles. Film theorists in the 1970s, in turn, rejected Bazin's beliefs about the medium's most important properties while also drawing on a new set of theoretical principles that questioned social and psychological norms more generally. Even as film theory cohered around the influence of French theory in the 1970s, much of the ferment of this period was rooted in the array of ongoing debates and dissenting factions that flourished. For instance, as briefly noted in Chapter 3, part of *Screen*'s editorial board resigned in protest against its theoretical direction and its unwillingness to tolerate opposing views. In addition to this internal turmoil, *Screen* was simultaneously attacked from both sides of the political spectrum. More conventional film critics decried the journal and its theorists as a form of intellectual terrorism.[1] Meanwhile, contemporary critics associated with journals like *Jump Cut* criticized *Screen* and its theoretical focus as a betrayal of its political radicalism.[2]

In some ways, the criticism directed at theory that emerged in the 1980s and 1990s was merely a continuation of this general pattern. Theory's critics were questioning the tenets that had, over the course of the previous generation, become the discipline's defining principles. But some of this questioning was clearly more than just healthy skepticism. The criticism that eventually culminated with *Post-Theory* often took on an ugly and more intense tone. To some extent, there is a correlation between this growing animosity and film study's formal establishment within the academy. Within the university system, for example, certain institutional pressures become more prominent and these tend to fuel a zero-sum mentality. Theory's critics, in this regard, were not just questioning the intellectual merit of established positions but also attacking the positions they believed had accrued a privileged status within the discipline. As part of a zero-sum mentality, the privileged status of certain positions necessarily means that other positions are rejected or marginalized. This mentality has meant that many debates about film theory have been loaded with personal and professional dimensions that complicate their overall scholarly significance.

While the publication of *Post-Theory* marks the point at which this antipathy reached a critical mass, many of its key points had been developing for some time. For instance, Noël Carroll's 1982 review of Stephen Heath's *Questions of Cinema* was one of the earliest and most emblematic examples of the claims taken up by theory's critics. As part of a review that spans over seventy pages, Carroll quickly establishes his intention to mount a wholesale attack on what he terms, in the book-length account that followed, the "dominant form of film theory" (*Mystifying Movies* 2). Throughout the review, there are essentially three chief issues that concern Carroll. First, he questions the emphasis that Heath (and, by extension, all of film theory) puts on French theory. In a preliminary sense, Carroll takes exception to the way Heath makes reference to these other thinkers. Like most film theorists, Carroll writes, "Heath does not give his readers the argumentative justifications for the basic philosophical presuppositions in his book," and this is in large part because he assumes readers "are familiar with, understand, and agree with the basic tenets of the Lacanian-Althusserian position" ("Address to the Heathen" 91). It is fairly clear, however, as Carroll lays siege to more specific terms like "perspective" and "suture," that no amount of exposition would have helped Heath's case. Carroll contends that these points have been fundamentally misconceived in part because of his second main concern. In his assessment, the most glaring problem for film theory lies in its assumptions about human subjectivity. He rejects in particular the ways in which both psychoanalysis and ideological interpellation frame human subjectivity as passive and inert. This is all the more problematic in that these views allow film theorists to overstate the illusory qualities associated with the cinematic image. He counters that this version "flies in the face of even casual observation. People do not mistake films for actual chains of events. The whole institution of film—with its emphasis on stars, the acquisition of new properties, etc.—is based on the audience's knowledge that films involve processes of production" ("Address to the Heathen" 99).

Carroll's third, and in many ways harshest, critique concerns the style of Heath's prose. This was something of a moot point by this time, yet it was (and remains) the easiest and most effective line of attack against theory. It was easy to point to select passages and lambaste them for their opaqueness. These examples then serve to dismiss entire arguments and as a way to ridicule theory as a whole. It is here that Carroll's account moves beyond mere evaluation and takes on a more baroque tone. For example, in the kind of passage that theory's subsequent critics latched onto, he writes:

> The style of *Questions of Cinema* is dense. The book is packed with neologisms, pleonasms, misuses, and strained uses of words and grammar—Heath, one surmises, enjoys calling things by the wrong name—and the book has strong tendencies toward formulaic repetition and belletristic rambling. If *Questions of Cinema* fails to become a favorite of graduate film students, this will undoubtedly be a consequence of its prose style. Throughout, the tone of the book is bullying. Heath liberally peppers his commentary with *thus*, and *therefore*—words that ordinarily signal the conclusion of a piece of reasoning—where there is no argument in the vicinity. The reader searches for nonexistent premises until he gives up—staring blankly at the poker-faced text. Heath also tends to overuse words like *precisely* and *exactly* at just those points in the exposition where he is least precise and exact.
>
> ("Address to the Heathen" 153)

It is certainly the case that theoretical writing can be inhospitably abstruse or turgid in ways that cover over imprecise claims. Carroll's condemnation, however, tends to overstate the role of style in general, suggesting that anything less than impeccable prose is tantamount to bad thinking. It also dismisses the performative dimensions implicit in the strategies associated with *écriture* and political modernism more generally. At the same time, Carroll's attack is not without its own rhetorical embellishments. He makes exaggerated generalizations and disparaging jabs when they suit his needs. Considering that "stylistic flourishes are *antithetical to the task of theorizing*," these asides betray Carroll's calls for a more measured and precise approach to theoretical discourse ("Address to the Heathen" 155).

For Heath, the review illustrates a shift in the overall frame of reference. First, he notes that there is some irony in Carroll's review appearing in *October*, a journal named after Sergei Eisenstein's film and that much like *Screen* took as its pretense a belief that "revolutionary practice, theoretical inquiry and artistic innovation" were inextricably intertwined.[3] More generally, Heath suggests that this type of attack is a clear effort to neutralize and de-politicize film theory as a practice: "In the new conservatism of the '80s, film theory, like so much else, is going to be brought to order, straightened out for academic discipline; what got into the academy is going to be got out; enough is enough" ("Le Père Noël" 112). To some extent Carroll would agree. He advocates for a new direction based on stricter logical standards and a different understanding of human subjectivity—one that rejects the problems and uncertainties associated with psychoanalysis. Heath, by contrast, associates this new direction with the rejection of ideology as a critical lens and an abandonment of film's political implications. In addition to this, Heath questions the nature of an exchange that he disparages as "pathetic male jockeying" ("Le Père Noël" 65). Like a number of the other intractable exchanges that took place in *Screen*, *Cinema Journal*, and elsewhere, the back and forth between Heath and Carroll could certainly be described as grappling; a decidedly male form of hand-to-hand combat consisting of clinching, pummeling, and coercing submission through the force of one's mass.[4] Despite being physically exhausting, there is little to show in terms of actual consequence. By the end, these debates were in most cases largely fruitless. In this respect, they evoke another failed encounter, one in which the efficacy of epistolary exchange was more generally called into question. As Jacques Derrida put it in an unsettled debate regarding Edgar Allan Poe's "The Purloined Letter," sometimes a letter does not reach its destination. Despite stirring a great deal of consternation, this seemed to be the case as the exchanges between theorists and their critics often ended at an impasse.[5]

The polemical nature of these exchanges tended to divert focus away from actually developing alternative theoretical methods. Carroll, for instance, makes several references to an alternative understanding of human subjectivity in his review of Heath but these are mainly used in a rhetorical fashion. "Why," he asks, "are no cognitive or perceptual structures included in Heath's model of film reception when it seems so painfully clear that some such mechanisms must come into play when audiences recognize a given film as coherent? If Heath believes that these structures are inadequate to the task at hand, he owes the reader an explanation why" ("Address to the Heathen" 131). The fact that Heath does not disprove the validity of competing scientific explanations is taken as further evidence of his inadequacy, but this does little to elaborate how or why these alternative explanations warrant further attention. As a result, they largely fell to the wayside as various rebuttals focused on the motivating logic of these attacks rather than the merits of what seemed to be passing rhetorical questions.

Although Carroll did not fully elaborate the parameters for an alternative method, his references to a more empirical-based approach to human subjectivity did serve as a point of departure for subsequent efforts. Over the course of the 1980s and 1990s, several scholars adopted cognitive science as the basis for this new approach. Their central presumption is that humans are rational creatures. Subsequently, emphasis is placed on the mental activities that take place as part of the viewing experience. While cognitive science refers to the study of mental activities in general, it is also a broad framework that allows for multiple sub-fields and different methodological undertakings. For example, cognitive science encompasses cognitive psychology, which tends to focus more specifically on mental faculties like memory, perception, and attention. In this regard, film scholars adopted **cognitivism** or cognitive theory to emphasize that this approach does not entail a unified or comprehensive theory, but rather a "perspective" or "frame of reference."[6] According to David Bordwell, the main concern of this perspective is "how spectators make sense of and respond to films" in conjunction "with the textual structures and techniques that give rise to spectatorial activity and response" ("Cognitive Film Theory" 24).

As part of this approach, it is assumed that the mind adheres to a formal logic and that it is possible to discern the pertinent computational procedures with regard to how individuals process sensory data. Although more recent research has broadened this approach to consider spectatorship in terms of neuroscience, it initially focused on the hypothetical relationship between spectators and films. The main task in this respect is to examine how spectators process the information provided as a matter of deductive reasoning. And this entails a kind of reverse engineering: the spectator's mental activities are extrapolated based on the information encoded as part of the film and the assumption that spectators observe standard problem-solving protocols in their approach to this information. At the same time that cognitivism provides flexibility in terms of how to extrapolate the relevant mental processes, this approach generally works in tandem with the principles of analytic philosophy. This means that cognitive theorists, as Carl Plantinga explains it, "are committed to clarity of exposition and argument and to the relevance of empirical evidence and the standards of science (where appropriate)" ("Cognitive Film Theory" 20). References to analytic philosophy, in other words, serve to establish logical positivism as a priority regardless of the specific research topic or interests. More generally, this approach insists that theory adhere to a more scientific style of discourse, privileging logical argumentation and empirical verification.

One area in which this approach has proven especially productive is narrative comprehension. Following his work in detailing the historical and aesthetic basis of classical Hollywood cinema, David Bordwell incorporated several key principles from cognitivism as part of his 1986 book, *Narration in the Fiction Film*. The premise for this study is twofold. First, he adopts a constructivist theory of visual perception drawn from psychology and Hermann von Helmholtz. This not only assumes that humans are rational beings, but also that as spectators they are actively engaged in the meaning-making process. Mental activities such as "perceiving and thinking" are in this view "active, goal-oriented processes" (*Narration* 31). And as a result, sensory data does not alone determine its significance. Instead, its significance is constructed in this case by the viewer through different cognitive operations—inferences supplemented by certain expectations and background knowledge, among other things. As part of this dynamic psychological process, viewers draw upon schema, what Edward Branigan defines as "an arrangement of knowledge *already possessed* by a perceiver that is used to predict and classify new sensory data" (*Narrative Comprehension* 13). This occurs both in a local and a general sense. Viewers make hypotheses about the specific events within a film based on familiarity or some measure of probability. They also approach narrative as whole in a schematic sense; they approach it as an existing repertoire of prototypes, templates, and patterns. In this regard, Bordwell establishes what he considers a kind of default position for film viewing. As a matter of comprehending narrative film, "the spectator seeks to grasp the filmic continuum as a set of events occurring in the defined settings and unified by principles of temporality and causation" (*Narration* 34).

Having established the active nature of spectatorship, the remainder of the book shifts to Bordwell's second premise regarding the function of film form and style. These are the cues that set up and determine the viewers' ability to formulate hypotheses, make inferences, and mobilize existing knowledge. As such, they indicate how the selection and arrangement of story materials, what Bordwell defines as **narration**, aims to engage viewers by both activating and modifying existing schema. To illustrate, Bordwell details how discrepancies between story and plot serve to "*cue* and *constrain* the viewer's construction of a story" (*Narration* 49). For instance, in a film that begins with the discovery of a murder victim, the viewer expects the story to include events that transpire both before and after the crime. The film, however, may choose to present these events in a way that constrains the viewer's ability to accurately make sense of the information provided. Narrative cinema does this primarily by retarding or delaying the revelation of important story material. As part of this process the viewer continues to construct hypotheses, which are then either confirmed or negated. Although this process foregrounds the film's ability to control information, it also confirms for Bordwell the active skill that spectatorship requires. As viewers are forced to revise and reconstruct their hypotheses, they become attuned to "a wider repertoire of schemata." When submitted to new data and additional variations, this prompts the viewer to develop "perceptual and conceptual abilities [that are] more supple and nuanced" (*Narration* 31).

Bordwell's approach to narration provided an important early step in establishing cognitivism as an alternative to the theoretical principles that took precedence throughout most of the 1970s and 1980s. Since 1986, scholars like Carl Plantinga, Richard Allen, Greg M. Smith, Gregory Currie, Murray Smith, and Torben Grodal have significantly advanced the field of cognitive film theory. In addition to incorporating cognitivism, Bordwell's account of narration draws attention to how form and style vary in conjunction with different historical and industrial circumstances. While virtually all forms of narrative cinema regulate the range of information available to viewers, there can be more significant variations in the degree of self-consciousness or communicativeness that they exhibit in doing so. This is commonly illustrated by contrasting Hollywood cinema, which varies in its degree of self-consciousness but invariably values communicativeness to maximize the number of potential viewers, with European art cinema, which in some cases minimizes or eliminates spatiotemporal cues to a point where it is difficult to discern causation. Bordwell further elaborates these variations by contrasting narrative films from different historical contexts, emphasizing that comprehension varies since schema—the prototypes, templates, and patterns drawn on to understand narrative—are determined socially. This also serves to introduce **historical poetics**, one of the other major developments in the post-theory period and a point of increasing emphasis throughout Bordwell's later work.

This new paradigm is often clearest in studies devoted to individual directors or national cinemas, for example Bordwell's book on Yasujiro Ozu or his survey of popular Hong Kong cinema. In terms of an exact definition, however, poetics proves somewhat elusive. The explanation that Bordwell most frequently offers is that poetics "studies the finished work as the result of a process of construction" while placing a corresponding emphasis on a work's specific "functions, effects, and uses" ("Historical Poetics" 371). The term "historical" serves to indicate, along the lines demonstrated in *Narration and the Fiction Film*, that these parameters change according to historical context. The challenge comes in distinguishing poetics from certain critical practices—Bordwell says poetics offers explanations whereas other practices merely furnish explications—while also accommodating synonymous terms like **neoformalism**. This latter term highlights the association between poetics and the emphasis that Bordwell and colleagues like Kristin Thompson place on rigorous formal analysis. While not wanting to dismiss the importance of such skills, Bordwell maintains that poetics cannot be reduced to a method of analysis. In another definition, he describes neoformalism as "a set of assumptions, an angle of heuristic approach, and a way of asking questions. It is frankly empirical and places great emphasis on the discovery of facts about films" ("Historical Poetics" 379). Despite this wavering, Bordwell does specify that there is an historical imperative at stake in this approach. As he reminds readers in *Narration and the Fiction Film*, "A little formalism turns one away from History, but a lot brings one back to it."[7] Although this reference is drawn from one of the members of what Bordwell later designated SLAB theory (a disparaging acronym for Saussure, Lacan, Althusser, and Barthes), it is meant to emphasize the difference between poetics and the abstractness of other theoretical models.

While Bordwell has produced numerous examples illustrating the merits of his poetical approach, his most interesting case for historical poetics is made somewhat indirectly in his book *Making Meaning*. In this instance he posits poetics as an antidote not only to theory but also to what he argues is a more widespread mode of fallible interpretation. To make this case, Bordwell outlines a history of writing on film whereby critics are beholden to a number of routine practices and formulaic conventions. Not entirely unlike the way viewers approach narrative cinema, Bordwell suggests that critics draw upon semantic fields in formulating hypotheses and ascribing meaning to film. He further details how interpretation changes over time with the dominant semantic field shifting from an artist–centered model (e.g. auteur criticism) in the 1950s and early 1960s to a form of symptomatic criticism that has reigned since the 1970s. In this regard, he reclassifies what generally constitutes theory as a series of interpretative conventions tailored to the requirements of a specific institutional context. To the extent that certain terms have become overused and certain figures have accrued a doctrinaire influence, he contends that this mode of interpretation has ceased to serve any kind of useful purpose. On the contrary, in fact, it has become conservative, a regulatory mechanism designed to subsume anything unfamiliar within an existing semantic field or set of heuristic protocols. And, "As if all this weren't enough," Bordwell finally adds, "it has become boring" (*Making Meaning* 261).

In the end, Bordwell returns to poetics as a way to escape both the failures of this interpretative paradigm and the misapplication of theory in general. As part of this move, he simultaneously establishes a more pronounced emphasis on historical scholarship. Though historical inquiry does not necessarily sidestep all of the vicissitudes of interpretation, it has the potential to generate a "more complex, precise, and nuanced" framework. In turn, such scholarship is "more likely to capture fresh and significant aspects" of film's function, effect, and uses (*Making Meaning* 266). This has certainly been the case with the immensely productive turn to early cinema that began in the 1980s and that accelerated in the 1990s as film theory took a backseat to other interests. In several instances, this new work also calls into question the strict divide between theory and history. For example, *Tom Gunning*'s notion of the **cinema of attractions** not only illuminates the specificity of early modes of film exhibition but has also been used to advance a variety of different scholarly interests.

The success of this scholarship highlights the extent to which the post-theory period has been one of ongoing growth and development. While the turn to cognitivism and historical poetics is often situated in direct opposition to theory, this was not always or necessarily the case. There were many ways in which these different directions, despite the antagonistic rhetoric, mutually benefitted the larger field of film study. For instance, historical inquiry was to a certain extent made possible only after film theory helped to establish the discipline within the academy. It was only after the field's intellectual merit had been formally recognized, in other words, that it then became prudent to return to previously overlooked areas of research. In turn, the revelations generated through historical inquiry prompted new efforts to reexamine neglected theoretical traditions. For instance, it was at this time that Vivian Sobchak inaugurated a return to phenomenology while Warren Buckland used the cognitive turn as an occasion to introduce a number of contemporary European theorists who combined cognitive science with film semiotics. In a broader sense, this is what D. N. Rodowick describes as a "metacritical or metatheoretical" turn within the discipline. As part of this development, scholars like Bordwell began "to exhibit fascination with the history of film study itself," and then to reconsider "problems" within its established methodologies ("Elegy for Theory" 95).

In one respect, the developments of the post-theory period are evidence of an evolving discipline, the benefits of institutional support, and the increasing rigor of the overall field. Despite these positive effects, there are also several points at which the differences between film theory and its critics are utterly irreconcilable and where debate has become totally unproductive. This is evident, for example, in the extreme position that Carroll offers in the conclusion to his book-length critique *Mystifying Movies*. Theory, he states, "has impeded research and reduced film analysis to the repetition of fashionable slogans and unexamined assumptions. New modes of theorizing are necessary. We must start again" (234). For many scholars, this completely disregards the achievements of feminist film theory, post-colonial theory, and queer theory. Moreover, it diminishes their interest in issues of power, difference, and identity and their calls for new counter-hegemonic forms of representation, suggesting that these frameworks lack rigor and are somehow inimical to logical positivism or evidence-based argumentation. In other words, these matters fall outside the realm of "real" scholarship and "legitimate" theory. In addition to broadly discrediting all film theory, Carroll's extreme position in *Mystifying Movies* begins to parallel some of the reactionary rhetoric taken up by cultural conservatives. This became explicit in his introduction to *Post-Theory*, where he condemns the political correctness of film theorists, asserting that this aims to protect "shoddy thinking and slapdash scholarship" while enforcing a conformist agenda that demands involuntary self-censorship (*Post-Theory* 45). In this regard, some post-theory sentiments evoke a much deeper antipathy for theoretical endeavors, for instance the Anglo-American rejection of esoterica as part of a broader Puritanical temperament and what Alexis de Tocqueville identified as America's deep suspicion of speculative inquiry or anything else without immediate practical application.[8]

With its emphasis on logical reasoning and empirical evidence, many took this new direction to be a rejection of the social and political associations that had played a prominent role in film theory's rise. And, by extension, many took this as an injunction against theory altogether. In response, Bordwell and Carroll offered a tenuous solution. They claimed they were not against theory but only Grand Theory, the variation of theory that had assumed an absolute position of infallibility throughout film study. Theory with a lower-case "t," by contrast, encompasses what they variously refer to as a "middle-level," "small-scale," "problem-driven," "moderate," "catholic," "piecemeal," and "bottom-up" approach to theorizing. This, of course, is the same kind of programmatic binary logic that Peter Wollen had recourse to in his earlier distinction between dominant cinema and counter-cinema: one is a good object that should be emulated and the other is a bad object that should be abhorred. The other problem with this distinction is that it tends to overstate the status of even the most influential strands of French theory. It was certainly the case that certain theoretical concepts had gained prominence in film theory's formative stages, but this is a far cry from saying that these theories were universally accepted or that they had assumed a hegemonic standing across the discipline.

As a corrective to the monolithic reign of Theory, Bordwell and Carroll call not just for a more modest version of theory but also for a profusion of these theories. There should be more quarreling, says Bordwell: "Dialogue and debate hone arguments" (*Making Meaning* 263). This sounds like an admirable call to further advance the field of film study, but the underlying logic is suspect. In a certain way, this call evokes the de-centering pluralism of post-modernism and post-structuralism. Is this, perhaps, an unwitting example of duplicity on their part? There were certainly instances in which Bordwell or Carroll resorted to the kind of punning word play that they otherwise condemned. Consider the title of Carroll's review of Heath's *Questions of Cinema*, "Address to the Heathen," a rather tactless reference designed more to rile up an adversary than to "hone arguments." But Bordwell and Carroll associate post-modernism and post-structuralism with Theory, which they have no interest in replicating in any way. The call for more vigorous theoretical debate isn't disingenuous, but it does suggest a more fundamental problem in trying to distinguish Theory from post-theory. In a certain way, their position recalls the structural logic of what political theorist Giorgio Agamben, in a very different context, describes as a "state of exception." Bordwell and Carroll call for a proliferation of theories only insofar as certain premises remain beyond questioning. In their view, more debate and more theory is welcome as long as one does not question basic assumptions like logical positivism, empirical evidence, or the rationality of human subjectivity. It isn't that these are invalid assumptions or that the scholarship that adheres to them has nothing to offer film theory. But this mentality does at times contribute to an ugly dynamic in which different sides refuse to recognize their common interests and their relationship to a larger institutional structure of knowledge production.

DELEUZE AND THE RETURN OF PHILOSOPHY

Even as some of the debates surrounding *Post-Theory* suggested that theory had entered into a debilitating state of crisis, the field continued to produce a broad array of theoretically based scholarship. Some of this shifted its focus to Bordwell and Carroll's "middle-level" approach or to historical inquiry more generally, but a good deal of it simply continued under the guise of Screen Theory. One new area of interest that developed at this time was the re-emergence of philosophy and, more specifically, the work of **Gilles Deleuze**. Deleuze was a major figure within the French theory tradition and, for many, is best known for his 1972 book, *Anti-Oedipus: Capitalism and Schizophrenia*, co-written with his frequent collaborator Félix Guattari. Partly because of that book's rejection of psychoanalysis, Deleuze found little favor among film theorists in the 1970s and 1980s. It became more difficult, however, to completely ignore Deleuze following the appearance of his own in-depth examination of cinema in *The Movement-Image* and *The Time-Image*. With D. N. Rodowick's 1997 account of these two books, film studies began a more serious consideration of this work and, since then, Deleuze has been an important touchstone in developing new theoretical interests.

What's both challenging and refreshing about Deleuze's approach to cinema is that he casts aside virtually all of the theoretical models introduced throughout the 1970s and 1980s. He instead sets out to study the medium as a whole, renewing the approach undertaken by earlier theorists and the general question, "What is cinema?" Deleuze, in response, isolates a series of cinematographic concepts or types of images, which taken together serve as a taxonomy that changes over time. The two broadest categories are the movement-image and the time-image, the two image types that are used to draw a distinction between cinema in the first and second half of the twentieth century and that also act as titles for the two volumes that make up Deleuze's study. Throughout the books, he illustrates these distinctions with detailed examples from various films and filmmakers, treating them as figures that think with images instead of concepts.

In terms of defining the movement-image, Deleuze argues that cinema emerges only as the image comes to signify more than a series of isolated or static units. In this respect, cinema begins not with the invention of moving images in 1895, but with the emergence of formal techniques like montage editing and the mobile camera. Both of these techniques form individual images that foster a different relationship to that which constitutes the whole. These images are no longer subordinate to an abstract sense of wholeness, but, rather, they open up this larger dimension in a qualitatively different way. For example, the mobile camera allows for dynamic reframing that engenders a tension between the image and its off-screen space. "All framing determines an out-of-field," according to Deleuze, "a larger set, or another set with which the first forms a larger one, and which can in turn be seen, on condition that it gives rise to a new out-of-field, etc." (*Cinema 1* 16). The individual shot is part of a larger whole that cannot be totalized. It is instead like a "thread which traverses sets and gives each one the possibility, which is necessarily realized, of communicating with another, to infinity. Thus the whole is the Open, and relates back to time or even to spirit rather than to content and to space" (*Cinema 1* 16–17).

Deleuze develops this approach by drawing on the work of Henri Bergson, another French philosopher who had fallen outside of film study's purview. According to Deleuze's reading, terms like "the whole" and "the Open" are associated with what Bergson identifies as duration, time, and consciousness. These categories resist scientific rationality, meaning they cannot be reduced to isolated static units within an abstract system of measurement. In associating cinema with these categories, Deleuze further associates it with what Bergson terms creative evolution. In this regard, cinema has the capacity to act like a consciousness in which "The whole creates itself, and constantly creates itself in another dimension without parts—like that which carries along the set of one qualitative state to another, like the pure ceaseless becoming which passes through these states" (*Cinema 1* 10). To return to the example of reframing, each individual shot opens an indeterminate possibility, "a universe or a plane of genuinely unlimited content." This plane is also described in terms of immanence, with the "capacity to open itself on to a fourth dimension which is time" (*Cinema 1* 17). In Rodowick's assessment, this is the most important part of Deleuze's engagement with cinema. While Deleuze's larger objective may be "to understand how aesthetic, philosophical, and scientific modes of understanding converge in producing cultural strategies for imagining and imaging the world," he is especially concerned with the question of time and how its shifting status is evident in the relationship between cinema and thought (*Gilles Deleuze's Time Machine* 5–6).

Although cinema's conceptual potential is evident throughout Deleuze's account of the movement-image, many of these strategies eventually came to be controlled by dominant commercial cinemas like Hollywood. Within the confines of such a system, these strategies become stagnant and conventional. In his second book, Deleuze turns his attention to the emergence of the time-image, the type of image in which cinema's potential is more fully apparent. This new image emerges in the aftermath of World War II, and it is primarily associated with European art cinemas like neorealism and the French new wave. The time-image is initially linked to a number of new formal and thematic elements. For example, Deleuze shows that films are more dispersed, spatial and temporal linkages are weakened, there is a greater emphasis on existential trips, there is an awareness of cliché, and there is less emphasis on plot.

More generally, he observes that post-war cinema is characterized by a growing sense of indeterminacy and by the impotency of human agency. However, these characteristics simultaneously allow for aberrant relations that render time directly visible. The time-image, in turn, takes on a different relationship to thinking. In Deleuze's words, "The sensory-motor break makes man a seer who finds himself struck by something intolerable in the world, and confronted by something unthinkable in thought. Between the two, thought undergoes a strange fossilization, which is as it were its powerlessness to function, to be, its dispossession of itself and the world" (*Cinema 2* 169). On its surface this may seem disconsolate, but for Deleuze this illustrates the potential of thought as "a force that continually renews the possibilities for change and the appearance of the new" (*Gilles Deleuze's Time Machine* 83). Following World War II, it was only by confronting the paralysis of thought that we might restore our relationship to the world and imagine the possibility of a future. Despite generally disregarding questions of power and difference, it was on this basis that subsequent scholars have taken up Deleuze as providing a model for a "minor cinema" capable of bringing into being those who have been excluded.

Following the initial delays in his reception, Deleuze has attracted growing attention among film theorists and his work has opened up new ways of exploring the relationship between philosophy and media. More broadly, his arrival corresponds with a greater willingness among both film scholars and philosophers to engage in common interests. One of the most prominent figures in this period has been Slavoj Žižek, a Lacanian cultural theorist known for his audacious ability to put Continental philosophy in conversation with popular culture. Others like Friedrich Kittler, Paul Virilio, and, more recently, Jacques Ranciere and Alain Badiou have also considered cinema from a more philosophical perspective. While these thinkers represent very different approaches, they are emblematic of a growing convergence between theory and philosophy. Deleuze concludes *Cinema 2* with a comment that both addresses this particular relationship and serves as a rejoinder to theory's critics. He writes that,

> The usefulness of theoretical books on cinema has been called into question . . . However, this remark does not show a great understanding of what is called theory. For theory too is something which is made, no less than its object. For many people, philosophy is something which is not "made" but is pre-existent, ready-made in a prefabricated sky. However, philosophical theory is itself a practice, just as much as its object. It is no more abstract than its object. It is a practice of concepts, and it must be judged in the light of the other practices with which it interferes. A theory of cinema is not "about" cinema, but about the concepts that cinema gives rise to and which are themselves related to other concepts corresponding to other practices, the practice of concepts in general having no privilege over others, any more than one object has over others. It is at the level of the interference of many practices that things happen, beings, images, concepts, all the kinds of events. The theory of cinema does not bear on the cinema, but on the concepts of the cinema, which are no less practical, effective or existent than cinema itself.
>
> (*Cinema 2* 280)

NEW MEDIA AND POST-FILM THEORY

By the end of the twentieth century film theory faced another challenge as the medium began to fundamentally change. Although many of the conventions associated with cinema remain, the introduction of digital technologies provided new forms of production, distribution, and exhibition. In particular, these developments have contributed to the decline of film as a photochemically based analog medium. These technologies have also had a broader effect in terms of reshaping the media and entertainment industries and in expanding the overall ubiquity of moving images and related screen technologies. This has created an environment in which the boundaries between film, television, and other competing formats are beginning to blur. Meanwhile, the term **new media** signals the emergence of more recent formats like video games, interactive devices, and internet-based platforms, as well as multi-media installations and art exhibits, that tend to be positioned in opposition to cinema. The overall expansion of visual culture has enlarged the scope of what counts as film and media study, but it has also generated some consternation regarding which methods and institutional perspectives should have priority.

There have also been divided views regarding the overall significance of these new developments. While some scholars remain wary of these new technologies, others have enthusiastically embraced their transformative powers. In terms of theorizing what distinguishes new media and the digital image in particular, scholars tend to identify technical differences while also adopting a comparative approach. For example, Lev Manovich identifies distinct new media features like modularity, automation, and programmability to indicate how media functions more like computer data. In this regard, new media follows a different structural logic. It is defined by its ability to be translated into multiple formats. At the same time, Manovich introduces the term "transcoding" to illustrate the way that new media absorbs and reconceptualizes older cultural categories. In the process of becoming new media, cinema, for instance, has become a form of animation or "subgenre of painting," which reconceptualizes the history of the medium. Jay David Bolter and Richard Grusin introduce a similar idea with their term **remediation**, or the intensification of mediated exchange that takes place as old and new media attempt to both replace and reaffirm one another. This interest in comparing the dynamic relationship between different types of media has prompted broader attempts to reconsider earlier instances, as in Jonathan Crary's account of nineteenth-century visual technologies, in which new and old media practices converge.

The turn to new media and the specificity of new digital technologies corresponded with a growing interest in how audiences were engaging with these developments. Henry Jenkins introduced the idea of **convergence culture** to describe the general relationship between contemporary media and society. On one hand, this term refers to technological convergence (e.g. the ability to watch movies on different platforms such as television or the internet) and corporate convergence (e.g. the strategy used by major media conglomerates to integrate complementary business ventures), as well as the growing prevalence of transmedia storytelling (e.g. the deployment of select characters or story elements across multiple media

formats and platforms). On the other hand, Jenkins is primarily interested in what convergence means for audiences: the new forms of
participation and sense of community that have emerged alongside
new media's emphasis on interactivity and social networking. In a
certain sense, this approach stems from the cognitivists' reappraisal
of viewers, mainly that they are not merely passive dupes but active
participants, even, for Jenkins, capable of resistance, subversion, and
transgression through tactics like **textual poaching**. Despite the
emphasis on the benefits of this new era, there are also deep suspi-
cions that surround the digital image. Those who are critical of these
new technologies focus on the intense commercialization of new
formats like the internet as well as issues like surveillance and privacy.

While many scholars have embraced the newness associated with
new digital technologies, several scholars have deemphasized the
magnitude of this shift. This implies that film theory's existing principles and methods are still applicable even in a post-film world.
As part of his ongoing return to the work of André Bazin, **Dudley
Andrew**, for example, asserts that cinema "does not rise or fall with
technology. A cinema of discovery and revelation can employ any
sort of camera" (*What Cinema Is!* 60). Although Andrew concedes
that the proliferation of digital technologies has inadvertently diminished the taste for this type of discovery, he points to recent digital
films—Zhang-ke's *Still Life* (2006) and Werner Herzog's *Grizzly
Man* (2005)—to illustrate how global art cinema continues to invoke
Bazin's notion of realism. In a different type of example, David
Bordwell argues that contemporary Hollywood maintains the principles of classical narrative cinema regardless of the new camera and
editing techniques associated with digital technologies. Faster editing
and the increased use of mobile cameras may have intensified established practices, but, he stresses, they continue to "serve traditional
purposes" (*The Way Hollywood Tells It* 119).

Many of these new interests have resulted in productive scholarly
research. At the same time, however, these new directions recall
the angst associated with the post-theory debates, raising concerns
about the discipline's cohesiveness and its overall durability. Partly as
a rejection of these new directions, D. N. Rodowick responds that
"a discipline's coherence derives not from the object it examines,
but rather from the concepts and methods it mobilizes to generate

critical thought" (*Virtual Life* xi). This means that even in a post-film era, film theory remains important and need not alter its identity.

Rodowick continues his point by raising the stakes of medium specificity. To this end, medium specificity is not reducible to old frameworks like realism or formalism, though the intensity of those earlier debates and the uncertainty of film's status because of those debates is part of its distinct ontological status. His primary point of reference is Stanly Cavell's *The World Viewed*, a largely underappreciated work, which, together with Siegfried Kracauer's *Theory of Film*, Rodowick describes as the "last great work of classical film theory" (*Virtual Life* 79). In the definition he extrapolates from Cavell, Rodowick explains the ontology of film as an expression of "our being or being-in-the-world, not necessarily as film spectators, but rather as a condition expressed in photography and cinema as such. This is a manifestation of a mind recognizing something that has already happened to itself" (*Virtual Life* 63). This means that film is less about what it represents and more about the relationship it produces between itself and the world, and how that relationship resembles our own relationship to the world. In other words, film encounters the world in a way that is akin to our "subjective condition of modernity" (*Virtual Life* 63). What's more, the relationship that film makes palpable is simultaneously about temporality, the irrevocable passing of time, the nature of history. What we see in film is the past, a reminder that we will also one day be part of that past. "What we register and seek to overcome or redeem in looking at photographs and films is [this] temporal alienation." In certain cases, when these images ignite "a circuit flowing between an external, surface perception of things and an inward movement characterized by memory and subjective reverie," this becomes possible (*Virtual Life* 77).

By contrast, digital images are very different. Digital images have a fundamentally different relationship to the world and, as a result, change the cognitive process by which we perceive such images. This in turn entails a different set of relationships. Whereas film "holds us in a present relation to the past and sustains our belief in a past world through the qualities of automatic analogical causation, digital screens require us to acknowledge others through efficient communication and exchange: I think because I exist in a present time of exchange with others, who are not present to me in space"

(*Virtual Life* 179). Though cinema is still possible in the post-film age, this new type of relationship has become increasingly conspicuous. Digital media functions primarily as a form of communication whereby information is considered valuable only as a unit of exchange within the logic of continuous circulation.

It is precisely because of this shift that Rodowick places such emphasis on film theory. Film theory constitutes the body of thinking devoted to understanding the importance of film in its specificity. Insofar as that medium has ceased to exist, that body of thinking can tell us even more about both the complexity of what used to be and the degree of difference with regard to what has taken its place. As Rodowick puts it, even as film is remediated as digital images, "the main questions and concepts of film theory persist, and we should pay careful attention to how they define a certain history of thought, how they can be used to reexamine that history, and how they form the basis for a critical understanding of new media and old. And at the same time, the core concepts of film theory are being recontextualized in ways that extend and render more complex their critical powers" (*Virtual Life* 188). In direct opposition to so much of the post-theory animus that claims theory is on the wane, Rodowick contends that it has greater critical power now than ever before. The reason for this is that images, and the overwhelming spread of digital culture are certainly testament to this, are so deeply ingrained in our society and ability to think about society that it is no longer possible to think without images and, by extension, the history of thinking about film images. In this regard, film theory has much to offer not only film or media studies in particular, but the advance of philosophy, culture, and critical thinking more generally. The title of his follow-up book, *Elegy for Theory*, emphasizes his lament, in effect mourning film theory's premature dismissal and the field's failure to reinvent it as part of a larger intellectual project. However, he also invokes elegy in another sense, as a praise song: "To feel one's self at the end of something inspires reflection on its ends, which may imply a defensiveness toward past incarnations, nostalgia, and longing for better days, or anxiety before an uncertain future. However, times of uncertain ends and historical self-examination suggest another possible direction. 'The past of theory demonstrates that theory has a future'" (*Elegy* 207).

Film theory has changed significantly over the course of its 100-year history and it is difficult to know what form it might take in the future. It is clear that film theory is deeply intertwined with its object of study. It was film that motivated various thinkers, scholars, critics, and artists to ask fundamental questions: What is cinema? What does it do? Why does it matter? Throughout the history of film theory these questions have been answered in terms of aesthetics, psychology, culture, politics, and so on. But more importantly than that, the different ideas and writings that emerged about cinema provided a basic sense of knowledge—descriptions and explanations—that paved the way for additional debate, analysis, and thinking. This material was successful to the extent that it became part of a larger conversation. It resonated to the extent that it was able to say something that wasn't otherwise possible, articulating something that existing assumptions and cultural standards had fundamentally precluded. The fact that film has given way to cinema, moving images, and digital media more broadly means that film theory now finds itself in a strange predicament. It is a body of knowledge without an object, but, as Rodowick argues, this may make it all the more interesting as it moves forward.

In the same way that film theory has been deeply intertwined with its object of study, it is an intellectual discourse that is completely contingent on historical context. It has changed as the medium has changed, in particular as the industrial conditions of its production and distribution have changed as well as when, where, and how it has been viewed by theorists. It has changed as the theorists who have written it have changed. And it has changed as its readers have changed. Early theorists had the biggest challenge in terms of writing about a medium of questionable merit. Film theory today is part of an established academic field of study. In this regard, film theorists enjoy the benefits of institutional stability along with the support of a professional association and other academic resources. This also means that film theory is a very specialized scholarly discourse, one that is subject to idiosyncratic standards that make it obscure or inaccessible to the general public. Throughout much of the second part of the twentieth century film theory was also closely related to a number of social and political movements. There was a belief that it was possible to not only write about cinema but also to do so in a way that changed it for the better and in ways that contributed to broader forms of social progress. Film theory continues to transform and part of its continuing relevance will depend on its ability to come to terms with both its past and its present. As long as there are images, there will always be a reason for theory, but what that theory is able to do is up to those who take on that task.

SUMMARY

In the two decades following its successful assimilation into the academy, film theory has entered a new and sometimes perilous period. Growing concerns about reigning models and the influence of French theory more generally came to a crescendo as select scholars enjoined the field of film study to adopt new objectives and different theoretical frameworks. Widespread technological changes have also raised questions. As film gives way to digital media and as cinema is recast as a form of visual information, it is uncertain whether film theory will remain the dominant conceptual lens for the critical analysis of moving images. Some of these questions have been tempered by the emergence of new figures like Gilles Deleuze and by film theory's potential affinities for broader philosophical concerns.

Questions

1. What are the main objections to so-called Grand Theory? What new directions are proposed to take its place and what are the advantages of these new directions?
2. What is different about Gilles Deleuze's approach to cinema? Why were there initial reservations about his approach and why does his work now resonate so strongly with film theorists?
3. How do digital technologies call into question some of film theory's main principles?
4. How does the introduction of new media change cinema as a social practice? And how does it change the kinds of questions we ask about its philosophical implications?
5. Does film theory have a future? Why or why not?

NOTES

1 See Bolas (2009): 233.
2 See, for example, Rich, Kleinhans, and Lesage (1978).
3 "About October." *October* 1 (Spring 1976): 3.
4 See the exchange between Barry King (1987) and Bordwell (1988), between Peter Lehman (1997) and Bordwell (1998), and between Buckland (1989) and Carroll (1992).
5 See Muller and Richardson (1988).
6 See Bordwell (1989b).
7 See Barthes (1957): 112 for the original.
8 De Tocqueville, Alexis. *Democracy in America.* Trans. George Lawrence. New York: HarperPerennial, 1969. 459.

APPENDIX I
GLOSSARY OF KEY TERMS

acousmêtre: a figure within the storyworld who is heard but not seen. This position retains a special power within most narratives, but can be rendered vulnerable when voice and body are realigned.

anti-humanism: a position adopted by several post-war French theorists that questions or rejects the assumptions of Western philosophy, especially the sovereignty of the human subject as a rational, self-determining agent.

apparatus theory: a distinction adopted by critics of cinema's ideological function; cinema is considered an ideological apparatus based on its methods of representation and the spectatorial position it provides.

attraction: concept developed by Sergei Eisenstein; derived from popular entertainment (e.g. amusement parks or the circus) and used by Eisenstein to provoke an intense reaction among spectators.

aura: a distinctive feature found in art and associated with its unique existence in a particular place; ostensibly rendered obsolete following technological advances that allow most forms of culture to be reproduced on a mass scale.

authorship: the general assumption that a film's creative virtues can be attributed to its director.

avant-garde: an artistic vanguard or group of innovators explicitly dedicated to challenging social and aesthetic norms.

camp: a sensibility or style that emphasizes artifice and exaggeration; also a reading practice whereby queer audiences recognize ostentatious figures or qualities within popular entertainment; a form that simultaneously conveys defiance and affirmation.

carnivalesque: a cultural practice in which traditional hierarchies are inverted, provided an alternative model of pleasure and subversion; associated with Mikhail Bakhtin.

castration: psychoanalytic concept associated with the male child's inability to comprehend anatomical difference; also functions as a paternal threat designed to enforce hetero-normative social and sexual relations.

cinema of attractions: Tom Gunning's term for a tendency in early cinema to directly address spectators, inciting visual curiosity by foregrounding the novelty of cinematic technologies; the term is drawn from Sergei Eisenstein and has been applied to different genres ranging from experimental cinema to pornography.

cinephilia: an intense affection or love for the cinema and its effects.

classical Hollywood cinema: a historical distinction referring to the Hollywood studio system and its methods of production; also a stylistic distinction referring to narrative conventions that privilege cause-and-effect logic as a way to maintain spatial and temporal continuity.

close analysis: analysis devoted to explicating a text's formal elements and their related codes; in the case of film, this involves detailed, shot-by-shot examination of select sequences.

code: a set of conventions that inform the selection or combination of units within a discursive formation; a code does not have the same regulative force as *langue*, meaning that it functions in a less restrictive manner; cinema is simultaneously informed by many codes (e.g. narrative codes, stylistic codes, technical codes, gender codes, etc.).

cognitivism: an approach that uses different aspects of cognitive science in the analysis and theorization of moving images; emphasizes how spectators understand and respond to specific techniques; borrows certain principles from analytic philosophy in terms of prioritizing clarity of argument and empirical evidence.

commodity fetishism: the principle developed by Marx that commodities are infused with values or associations that exceed their basic material composition.

condensation: psychoanalytic term referring to an unconscious process, in dreams for example, whereby certain ideas are fused together.

connotation: associated meanings attached to or evoked by a sign; often specific to the sign's social and cultural context.

convergence culture: a general description of media and society in which older boundaries are dissolving and new relationships are emerging; this is apparent in terms of technology, industrial organization, and transmedia storytelling; but for Henry Jenkins it is most interesting in relation to the new forms of audience participation and fandom that have developed.

counter-cinema: oppositional style of filmmaking that rejects the dominant ideology at the level of both form and content.

cultural studies: academic field that parallels the emergence of film study in the 1970s; primarily associated with the British scholars at the Centre for Contemporary Cultural Studies at the University of Birmingham.

decoding: part of any communicative exchange in which an encoded messaged must be decoded by the receiver; in Stuart Hall's account, decoding can gravitate in different directions—it can adhere to the intended meaning of a message or it can negotiate or reject that meaning.

defamiliarization: a practice used to subvert or challenge common conventions by making them appear strange or unfamiliar.

denotation: literal or obvious meaning of a sign.

dialectical materialism: a Marxist concept that suggests material economic conditions form the basis of class struggle and the drive to fundamentally transform society; Soviet filmmakers applied to cinema, treating individual shots as film's material basis and montage as a means of putting them into conflict.

disavow: a form of denial or a defense mechanism adopted to avoid traumatic encounters or other objectionable realities.

displacement: psychoanalytic term referring to an unconscious process, in dreams for example, whereby certain ideas are rearranged and assigned to different but associated ideas.

écriture: style of writing developed by a group of intellectuals associated with *Tel Quel*, one of France's leading journals of the 1960s and 1970s; this style of writing adopted certain modernist techniques and rejected the imperative that communication need be utilitarian.

fantasy: an imaginary scenario that accommodates the desire for wish fulfillment; a widely discussed psychoanalytic concept that resonates with cinema's ability to generate fanciful situations.

fetishism: psychoanalytic concept that accounts for cases in which an individual maintains two incompatible beliefs at the same time—the primary example of this occurs when a male confronts a female's lack of a penis; the fetish object stands in for the absent penis, allowing the male to disavow both anatomical difference and castration anxiety; for Laura Mulvey, it is part of a containment strategy made necessary by the manner in which female characters evoke castration anxiety; in this case, it involves an extreme aestheticization of the cinematic image to the point that it suspends the threat of castration.

formalism: a general position that assumes film is primarily defined by its formal practices rather than its photographic realism.

Frankfurt School: a designation for German scholars formally or informally associated with the Institute of Social Research; though individual research varied widely, this school represents a general interest in culture, aesthetics, and philosophy.

grande syntagmatique: a categorization of narrative cinema's most common autonomous segments or sequential units developed by Christian Metz; the different units are classified according to their ordering logic and function—for example, there is a group that maintains chronological order and a group that doesn't; nonchronological syntagmas include scenes in which parallel editing brings two different events together without specifying their temporal relationship.

hegemony: explains how social control is cultivated through mutual consent rather than direct force; operates in conjunction with common sense whereby the ruling class dictates the ideals that all groups accept as self-evident.

historical poetics: study of cinema that emphasizes a work's specific functions, effects, and uses.

identification: psychological process in which an individual recognizes someone or something as similar to itself; Christian Metz draws a distinction between primary cinematic identification and secondary cinematic identification—in the former, the spectator identifies with the camera and, in the latter, the spectator identifies with characters based on real or perceived similarities.

Ideological State Apparatus: term introduced by Louis Althusser to explain why social institutions like family, religion, and the education system are more effective in maintaining the status quo than more repressive means (e.g. military or police forces).

ideology: the ideas, beliefs, or manner of thinking associated with a particular society or group within a society; in post-war French theory, more specifically refers to the naturalization of socially and culturally constructed distinctions and how that process supports the ruling class.

indexical: a type of sign identified by Charles Sanders Peirce and, more specifically, representations that share an existential bond with their referent. This designation has been used to explain the photochemical process that allows images to be recorded.

interpellation: the process by which individuals are constituted as subjects within a social system; Louis Althusser compares this to the misrecognition that occurs within the mirror stage and uses the example of a police officer "hailing" an innocent bystander.

jouissance: French term for enjoyment that also evokes a sexual pleasure that exceeds biological necessity; for French feminists, the term is used to indicate a form of female pleasure that exists outside of language or patriarchal repression.

langue: French term for language and sometimes translated as language system; refers to the abstract system of rules and conventions that determine *parole*, or the words that can be spoken by individuals within that system.

male gaze: the way in which Hollywood cinema aligns the viewer with male protagonists in looking at female characters as a passive or erotic object.

masochism: behavior in which satisfaction is derived from suffering or humiliation; initially, an overlooked alternative to sadism within feminist film theory.

masquerade: feminist strategy whereby it is understood that femininity is a culturally constructed façade, but it is also a pretense that can be appropriated as a form of female agency and as a means of resisting patriarchal assumptions about gender.

mass ornament: Siegfried Kracauer's term for a 1920s trend in which individuals were assembled into larger patterns as part of a marching band or dance performance; more generally, a figure that illustrates the contradictions within popular culture.

medium specificity: the idea that each art form possesses distinct qualities that are unique to its specific material properties and associated techniques.

mirror stage: psychoanalytic theory introduced by Jacques Lacan to explain human subjectivity; between the age of six and eighteen months, a child recognizes itself in the mirror as an independent and unified whole despite still lacking the necessary motor coordination skills necessary to function autonomously.

modernism: a general art movement that emerged in the early twentieth century and that featured different stylistic techniques designed to deconstruct or problematize conventional aesthetic practices.

montage theory: the emphasis on editing as the primary means of developing cinema's aesthetic and political potential; developed by Soviet filmmakers in the 1920s.

narration: the selection and arrangement of story materials to have a specific effect on viewers.

neoformalism: an approach that emphasizes rigorous formal analysis; inspired in part by Russian Formalists' approach to literature and closely related to David Bordwell's notion of historical poetics.

new media: term used to signal the emergence of more recent formats like video games, interactive devices, and internet-based technologies, as well as multi-media installations and art exhibits; these new formats tend to be positioned in opposition to cinema and television, which are considered older formats.

Oedipal complex: psychoanalytic theory in which children consider the parent of the same sex to be a rival while also developing a sexual desire for the parent of the opposite sex.

optical unconscious: Walter Benjamin's term for the way in which photography reveals unseen elements of the visible world; also evokes his ambivalence regarding the status of aura in film and technology's potential to reverse the negative effects associated with modern industrial society.

Orientalism: the practice whereby the Orient is constructed to reflect the West's attitudes and anxieties about the non-West; the Orient is presented as inferior, exotic, and backwards; Edward Said identifies in order to critique.

other: in Lacanian psychoanalysis the self/other dynamic evokes Hegel's master/slave dialectic; Lacan later draws a distinction between the little other or *objet petite a* and the big other or Other—the former suggests the persistence of otherness within the self, the latter is linked to language and the symbolic order; the term more generally refers to individuals or groups that have been socially and culturally marginalized due to racial or ethnic differences.

panopticon: an architectural design proposed by Jeremy Bentham in the eighteenth century and discussed by Michel Foucault in his analysis of the prison system and related disciplinary practices. The design allows for prisoners to be observed at any time without their knowing. This leads inmates to internalize a state of perpetual surveillance.

parole: French term for speech; Saussure uses it to identify the activity of individual speakers within a system of *langue*.

patriarchy: a social or cultural system of privilege whereby the male sex assumes priority over and as the basis for subordinating or oppressing the female sex; feminist film theorists analyze its discursive and structural functions in shaping Hollywood cinema and other forms of popular media.

phallus: whereas Freud uses phallus and penis somewhat interchangeably, Lacan treats the phallus as a paternal signifier that has only a tenuous relationship to its anatomical reference; the phallus still plays a central role in establishing traditional notions of sexual difference and maintaining a system of patriarchal privilege.

photogénie: a reference to something or someone that lends itself to photographic representation; term embraced by French filmmakers and critics in the 1920s to indicate cinema's unique revelatory powers.

plot: the arrangement or ordering of events as part of a narrative presentation; this presentation does not necessarily adhere to the chronological succession of events; sometimes used interchangeably with the Russian term, *syuzhet*.

poetics: form of literary analysis that examines particular texts as a way to extrapolate their governing formal properties.

political modernism: term developed by D. N. Rodowick to characterize the approach of many theorists and critics in the 1960s and 1970s; entails a general assumption that theory, politics, and art share an overlapping relationship and that they can be combined in certain ways to effect social change or subvert dominant ideologies.

la politique des auteurs: the concept of authorship as it emerged at *Cahiers du cinéma* in the 1950s; the idea that a film's director expresses a certain world view through stylistic devices or thematic patterns; a polemical challenge to existing assumptions about Hollywood cinema and critics' ability to interpret their significance.

post–modern: a term that refers to both a historical periodization and a stylistic movement—the former signifies a shift following World War II in which earlier cultural and political paradigms began to lose their efficacy; the latter is typically associated with the proliferation of simulations, pastiche, and blank irony.

post–structuralism: a movement away from the scientific undercurrents of structuralism and the growing interest in the 1960s in deconstructing the idea of fixed or stable structures.

Quattrocento: a technique that emerged as part of the Italian Renaissance that used linear perspective to create the illusion of depth in painting; the cinematic image adheres to this same system in its representational logic.

realism: a general position that assumes film is primarily defined by its photographic realism rather than its formal practices.

remediation: term introduced by Jay David Bolter and Richard Grusin to indicate the contradictory relationship between old and new media whereby the attempt to replace older formats ends up reaffirming them.

repression: the effort to confine select thoughts to the unconscious; certain thoughts and ideas are repressed because they are deemed socially unacceptable.

Russian Formalists: an informal group of intellectuals and scholars interested in the study of language and literature; the group includes figures ranging from Victor Shklovsky and Mikhail Bakhtin to Roman Jakobson.

sadism: psychoanalytic concept concerning taking pleasure from the experience of suffering and humiliation; for Laura Mulvey, part of a containment strategy made necessary by the manner in which female characters evoke castration anxiety.

semiotics (or semiology): the study of signs or sign systems.

sign: a unit of meaning that stands in for something else; Saussure equates the sign with an individual word, the smallest unit of meaning within language; signs can also refer to more complex formations like an individual image, which may combine multiple signs.

signified: the mental concept associated with a sign; Saussure divided the sign into two parts—the signified and the signifier—and showed that their relationship is arbitrary.

signifier: the spoken or written articulation of a sign; Saussure divided the sign into two parts—the signified and the signifier—and showed that their relationship is arbitrary.

story: the chronological order of events comprised within a narrative; sometimes used interchangeably with the Russian term, *fabula*.

structuralism: a broad intellectual movement that took root in post-war France and focused critical attention on the abstract structures and systems of relationships that condition the production of meaning.

surrealism: an art movement that began in France in the 1920s and that encourages the blending of dreams and reality.

suture: term drawn from Lacan's principle that subjectivity is constituted through discourse and used to explain how spectators are inserted into cinematic discourse in a way that also excludes them; evokes the surgical process in which a wound or absence is covered over.

symptomatic: the appearance of signs that indicate an underlying issue or problem; used in its adjective form to describe the manner in which cultural texts convey meaning.

textual poaching: a specific tactic associated with the reappraisal of viewers and their ability to be active participants, resisting or subverting film and media's intended uses.

third cinema: form of post-colonial counter-cinema conceived in opposition to both dominant commercial cinema and established art cinemas; rejects Euro-centrism and the legacy of imperialism.

to-be-looked-at-ness: the general tendency for women to function primarily as an erotic spectacle within Hollywood cinema; term introduced by Laura Mulvey as part of her analysis of how patriarchal ideology structures narrative cinema.

trauma: derived from the Greek term for wound; refers to events or experiences characterized by their intensity and overwhelming nature.

unconscious: psychoanalytic concept that designates the part of human subjectivity to which forbidden desires and other repressed materials are relegated.

voyeurism: the pleasure of seeing others or something forbidden while remaining unseen.

APPENDIX II
GLOSSARY OF KEY THEORISTS

Adorno, Theodor (1903–69): German intellectual and leading member of the Frankfurt School; best known in relation to film for his devastating critique (co-written with Max Horkheimer) of the culture industries as a ruthless extension of capitalist domination.

Althusser, Louis (1918–90): French theorist who initiated a renewed interest in Marx and is best known for emphasizing the role of ideology in maintaining the existing system of social relations; ideology, in his view, interpellates subjects into a system in which they are compelled to forfeit any ability to effect change.

Andrew, Dudley: Contemporary film scholar and key figure in the establishment of film studies as an academic discipline; leading advocate in the return to André Bazin's work and a more general reassessment of cinematic realism.

Arnheim, Rudolf (1904–2007): German-born scholar of art and psychology who advocated a formalist approach to cinema, believing that film's artistic potential rested in the formal techniques like editing that distanced the medium from its affinity for mimesis or realism.

Balázs, Béla (1884–1949): Hungarian film theorist best known for his account of the emotional and dramatic powers of the close-up.

Barthes, Roland (1915–80): French theorist who applied the tenets of structuralism to cultural and literary analysis; in *Mythologies*, he develops an analysis of second-order signifying practices whereby meaning is naturalized and the status quo reinforced.

Baudry, Jean-Louis: French writer and member of the editorial committee at *Tel Quel*; best known for a series of essays that condemn cinema as an ideological apparatus.

Bazin, André (1918–58): Key figure in post-war French film culture and theorist of cinematic realism; a co-founder of the influential journal *Cahiers du cinéma* and proponent of European art cinema who articulated the significance of movements like Italian neorealism.

Benjamin, Walter (1892–1940): German intellectual loosely associated with the Frankfurt School who gained prominence posthumously due to his unconventional approach to culture, art, and politics; he is best known for claiming that new technologies like film had eliminated aura as art's distinguishing feature.

Bhabha, Homi: Contemporary post-colonial theorist who explores the potential within hybrid identities and the interstitial spaces opened up through cultural difference.

Bordwell, David: Contemporary film scholar who has written extensively on classical Hollywood, individual filmmakers, and art cinema; his work draws attention to film's formal elements, characterizing this approach as historical poetics.

Brecht, Bertolt (1898–1956): German playwright best known for encouraging the use of alienation effects, techniques designed to expose established conventions and disrupt the pleasure associated with these conventions.

Breton, André (1896–1966): French writer and leader of the surrealist movement.

Butler, Judith: Contemporary queer theorist who argues that sex and gender are discursively constructed; these categories are constituted and maintained through the performance of gender norms; queer identities foreground the performativity implicit in these norms.

Carroll, Noël: Contemporary film theorist with a wide range of interests spanning from the philosophy of art in general to the emergence of cognitive sciences in the reappraisal of principles drawn from French theory.

Chion, Michel: Contemporary French film theorist who focuses on sound.

de Lauretis, Teresa: Contemporary theorist whose work engages the intersection between feminist film theory and queer theory; returns to psychoanalysis while also incorporating post-structuralism as part of these efforts.

Deleuze, Gilles (1925–95): French philosopher who addressed cinema in a two-book study published in the 1980s; though initially an outlier compared to other French theorists, his work provides an innovative new approach that opens cinema to new philosophical consideration; Deleuze is particularly interested in the relationship between cinema and time.

Delluc, Louis (1890–1924): An influential critic and filmmaker who played a significant role in developing France's film culture in the 1920s and in promoting concepts like *photogénie*.

Dulac, Germaine (1882–1942): A French filmmaker and critic who identified several of the stylistic features associated with cinematic impressionism.

Eisenstein, Sergei (1898–1948): Soviet film theorist and filmmaker who considered montage to be an extension of dialectical materialism and the best way to foster cinema's political and intellectual implications.

Epstein, Jean (1897–1953): A filmmaker and critic associated with France's film culture in the 1920s and the emergence of concepts like *photogénie*.

Foucault, Michel (1926–84): French philosopher who wrote on a wide range of topics related to power and discourse; his analysis of the prison system and disciplinary practices became well known for his discussion of the panopticon, a system in which prisoners can be observed at any time without their knowing.

Freud, Sigmund (1856–1939): Austrian founder of psychoanalysis, a clinical practice and collection of theories dedicated to the interpretation of the unconscious and other human behaviors.

Gramsci, Antonio (1891–1937): Italian Marxist and socialist activist known for his account of hegemony, which explains how social control is cultivated through mutual consent rather than direct force.

Gunning, Tom: Contemporary film scholar best known for his work on early cinema and specifically his notion of early cinema as a cinema of attractions—one that directly addresses spectators, inciting visual curiosity by foregrounding the novelty of cinematic technologies.

Hall, Stuart (1932–2014): British cultural theorist associated with the development of cultural studies.

Hansen, Miriam (1949–2011): Contemporary film scholar who prompted a return to the work of Walter Benjamin and Siegfried Kracauer and a general reassessment of the Frankfurt School's engagement with cinema.

Heath, Stephen: Contemporary film theorist associated with the British journal *Screen* and especially active in the 1970s; representative of that period's effort to bring together psychoanalysis, semiotics, and Marxist ideology critique through detailed narrative and formal analysis.

Jameson, Fredric: Contemporary Marxist theorist and philosopher who has written widely on culture, literature, art, and film.

Kracauer, Siegfried (1889–1966): German intellectual who wrote extensively about culture and society. After emigrating to the United States in 1941, he completed several book-length studies devoted to cinema. He tends to emphasize film's realist properties, but also considered its more dialectical nuances and its complex relationship to modern experience.

Kuleshov, Lev (1899–1970): Soviet filmmaker and theorist whose workshop at the Moscow Film School established the importance of montage; also known for the "Kuleshov effect," the principle that meaning is produced through the relationship between multiple shots.

Lacan, Jacques (1901–81): French psychoanalyst who incorporated structuralist linguistics, philosophy, and references to modern art in his return to Freud; best known for his theory of the mirror stage in which subjectivity is formed as part of the visual exchange that takes place when an infant first encounters their reflection.

Lévi-Strauss, Claude (1908–2009): French anthropologist and critical figure in launching structuralism; transposed the principles of structuralist linguistics to the study of cultural institutions like marriage rites and family structure across different social systems.

Lindsay, Vachel (1879–1931): American poet and author of one of the first book-length studies of cinema.

MacCabe, Colin: Contemporary film theorist associated with the British journal *Screen*; his account of the classic realist text is representative of a shift in focus away from issues related to medium specificity to a growing emphasis on discursive analysis.

Marx, Karl (1818–83): German political theorist who analyzed society as structured by class conflict; he developed influential views about history and economics, and advocated for a revolutionary overthrow of the capitalist system.

Metz, Christian (1931–93): French film theorist who thoroughly investigated the relationship between cinema and language; became interested in the syntagmatic organization of film and developed a taxonomy of common sequential units; after his initial focus on semiotic issues, Metz considered the relationship between cinema and psychoanalysis.

Mulvey, Laura: Contemporary feminist film theorist and filmmaker; her essay "Visual Pleasure and Narrative Cinema" marked an important turning point in film study, inaugurating intense debates about how the male gaze structures the female's function as an erotic spectacle and the possibility of creating an alternative cinema devoted to female spectators.

Münsterberg, Hugo (1863–1916): German-born Harvard professor of psychology and author of *The Photoplay: A Psychological Study*, which argues that film's formal operations parallel cognitive faculties like attention, memory, and imagination.

Nichols, Bill: Contemporary film theorist best known for drawing critical attention to documentary.

Peirce, Charles Sanders (1839–1914): American philosopher who gained posthumous attention with the rise of semiotics. He identified three types of signs: iconic, symbolic, and indexical. Indexical signs include representations that share an existential bond with their referent, a designation that has been used to explain the photochemical process in the recording of cinematic images.

Rodowick, D. N.: Contemporary film theorist who has written extensively about the influence of French theory and the formation of film study as a distinct theoretical discourse.

Sarris, Andrew (1928–2012): American film critic and popularizer of the auteur theory.

Saussure, Ferdinand de (1857–1913): Founder of modern linguistics and an important influence in the foundation of structuralism; drew attention to the sign as the smallest unit of meaning within language, an approach that served as a model for semiotics and the study of other sign systems.

Silverman, Kaja: Contemporary feminist film theorist who draws on Lacanian psychoanalysis to demonstrate that all cultural subjects experience symbolic castration.

Trinh T., Minh-ha: Contemporary theorist and filmmaker; joins post-structuralism with performative techniques in both her writing and filmmaking as a way to critique the implicit Eurocentrism within the university system.

Vertov, Dziga (1896–1954): Soviet filmmaker and theorist who celebrated the powers of what he termed the Kino-Eye, or cinema's ability to reveal and rethink modern life.

Williams, Linda: Contemporary feminist film theorist and scholar with a wide range of interests; well known for initiating the critical study of pornography.

Wollen, Peter: Contemporary film theorist associated with the British journal *Screen*. His book *Signs and Meaning* was one of the first to introduce Anglophone readers to the tenets of French Theory. He advocated for the development of a counter-cinema and went on to make several films with Laura Mulvey.

BIBLIOGRAPHY

CHAPTER 1: THEORY BEFORE THEORY, 1915–60

Abel, Richard, ed. *French Film Theory and Criticism: A History/Anthology, Volume I 1907–1939*. Princeton, NJ: Princeton University Press, 1988.

Aitken, Ian. *European Film Theory and Cinema: A Critical Introduction*. Bloomington, IN: Indiana University Press, 2001.

And'el, Jaroslav, ed. *Art into Life: Russian Constructivism, 1914–1932*. Seattle, WA: Henry Art Gallery, University of Washington, 1990.

Andrew, Dudley. *André Bazin*. New York: Columbia University Press, 1978.

Andrew, Dudley and Hervé Joubert-Laurencin, eds. *Opening Bazin: Postwar Film Theory and Its Afterlife*. New York: Oxford University Press, 2011.

Arnheim, Rudolf. *Film as Art*. Berkeley, CA: University of California Press, 1957.

Balázs, Béla. *Theory of the Film: Character and Growth of a New Art*. Trans. Edith Bone. New York: Dover, 1970.

——. *Béla Balázs: Early Film Theory*. Trans. Rodney Livingstone. Ed. Erica Carter. New York: Berghahn Books, 2010.

Bazin, André. *What Is Cinema? Volume I*. Trans. Hugh Gray. Berkeley, CA: University of California, 1967.

——. *What Is Cinema? Volume II*. Trans. Hugh Gray. Berkeley, CA: University of California, 1971.

——. *Jean Renoir*. Trans. W. W. Halsey II and William H. Simon. New York: Da Capo Press, 1973.

——. *Bazin at Work: Major Essays and Reviews from the Forties and Fifties*. Ed. Bert Cardullo. Trans. Alain Piette and Bert Cardullo. New York: Routledge, 1997.

Benjamin, Walter. *Illuminations*. Ed. Hannah Arendt. Trans. Harry Zohn. New York: Schocken, 1968.

——. *The Origin of German Tragic Drama*. Trans. John Osborne. New York: Verso, 1998.

——. *Walter Benjamin: Selected Writings, Volume 2, 1927–1934*. Eds. Michael W. Jennings, Howard Eiland, and Gary Smith. Cambridge, MA: Harvard University Press, 1999.

——. *Walter Benjamin: Selected Writings, Volume 3, 1935–1938*. Eds. Howard Eiland and Michael W. Jennings. Cambridge, MA: Harvard University Press, 2002.

——. *Walter Benjamin: Selected Writings, Volume 4, 1938–1940*. Eds. Howard Eiland and Michael W. Jennings. Cambridge, MA: Harvard University Press, 2003.

Bordwell, David. *French Impressionist Cinema: Film Culture, Film Theory, and Film Style*. New York: Arno Press, 1980.

——. *Narration in the Fiction Film*. Madison, WI: University of Wisconsin Press, 1985.

——. *The Cinema of Eisenstein*. New York: Routledge, 2005.

Bottomore, Tom, ed. *A Dictionary of Marxist Thought*. 2nd ed. Malden, MA: Blackwell, 1998.

Brecht, Bertolt. *Brecht on Theater: The Development of an Aesthetic*. Ed. and trans. John Willett. New York: Hill and Wang, 1992.

Breton, André. *Manifestos of Surrealism*. Trans. Richard Seaver and Helen R. Lane. Ann Arbor, MI: Ann Arbor Paperbacks, University of Michigan, 1972.

Carroll, Noël. "Film/Mind Analogies: The Case of Hugo Münsterberg." *The Journal of Aesthetics and Art Criticism*, Vol. 46, No. 4 (Summer 1988): 489–499.

——. "Medium Specificity Arguments and the Self-Consciously Invented Arts: Film, Video, and Photography." *Theorizing the Moving Image*. Cambridge: Cambridge University Press, 1996. 3–24.

Decherney, Peter. *Hollywood and the Culture Elite: How the Movies Became American*. New York: Columbia University Press, 2005.

Eisenstein, Sergei. *The Eisenstein Reader*. Trans. Richard Taylor and William Powell. Ed. Richard Taylor. London: BFI, 1998.

Epstein, Jean. *The Intelligence of a Machine*. Trans. Christophe Wall-Romana. Minneapolis, MN: Univocal, 2014.

Erlich, Victor. *Russian Formalism: History – Doctrine*. New York: Mouton Publishers, 1980.

Fredericksen, Donald. *The Aesthetic of Isolation in Film Theory: Hugo Münsterberg.* New York: Arno Press, 1977.

Grant, Barry Keith, ed. *Auteurs and Authorship: A Film Reader.* Malden, MA: Blackwell, 2008.

Hammond, Paul, ed. *The Shadow and Its Shadow: Surrealist Writings on the Cinema.* Trans. Paul Hammond. San Francisco, CA: City Lights Books, 2000.

Hansen, Miriam Bratu. *Cinema and Experience: Siegfried Kracauer, Walter Benjamin, and Theodor W. Adorno.* Berkeley, CA: University of California Press, 2012.

Higgins, Scott, ed. *Arnheim for Film and Media Studies.* New York: Routledge, 2011.

Hillier, Jim, ed. *Cahiers du Cinéma: The 1950s, Neo-Realism, Hollywood, New Wave.* Cambridge, MA: Harvard University Press, 1985.

Horkheimer, Max and Theodor W. Adorno. *Dialectical of Enlightenment: Philosophical Fragments.* Trans. Edmund Jephcott. Stanford, CA: Stanford University Press, 2002.

Jay, Martin. *The Dialectical Imagination: A History of the Frankfurt School and the Institute of Social Research, 1923–1950.* Boston, MA: Little, Brown and Company, 1973.

Keller, Sarah and Jason N. Paul, eds. *Jean Epstein: Critical Essays and New Translations.* Amsterdam: Amsterdam University Press, 2012.

Kracauer, Siegfried. *From Caligari to Hitler: A Psychological History of the German Film.* Princeton, NJ: Princeton University Press, 1947.

——. *The Mass Ornament: Weimar Essays.* Ed. and trans. Thomas Y. Levin. Cambridge, MA: Harvard University Press, 1995.

——. *Theory of Film: The Redemption of Physical Reality.* Princeton, NJ: Princeton University Press, 1997.

Kuenzli, Rudolf, ed. *Dada and Surrealist Film.* Cambridge, MA: MIT Press, 2001.

Kuleshov, Lev. *Kuleshov on Film: Writings of Lev Kuleshov.* Trans. and ed. Ronald Levaco. Berkeley, CA: University of California Press, 1974.

Lindsay, Vachel. *The Art of the Moving Picture.* New York: Modern Library, 2000.

MacDonald, Dwight. "A Theory of Mass Culture." *Mass Culture: Popular Arts in America.* Eds. Bernard Rosenberg and David Manning White. New York: Free Press, 1959.

Marcuse, Herbert. *One-Dimensional Man: Studies in the Ideology of Advanced Industrial Society.* Boston, MA: Beacon Press, 1964.

May, Lary. *Screening Out the Past: The Birth of Mass Culture and the Motion Picture Industry.* Chicago, IL: University of Chicago Press, 1980.

Mitchell, George. "The Movies and Münsterberg." *Jump Cut: A Review of Contemporary Media* 27 (July 1982): 57–60. www.ejumpcut.org/archive/onlinessays/JC27folder/Munsterberg.html.

Morgan, Dan. "Rethinking Bazin: Ontology and Realist Aesthetics." *Critical Inquiry* 32 (Spring 2006): 443–481.

Münsterberg, Hugo. *Münsterberg on Film*: The Photoplay: A Psychological Study *and Other Writings*. Ed. Allan Langdale. New York: Routledge, 2002.

Overbey, David, ed. *Springtime in Italy: A Reader on Neo-Realism*. Hamden, CT: Archon Books, 1979.

Peirce, Charles Sanders. *Peirce on Signs: Writings on Semiotic by Charles Sanders Peirce*. Ed. James Hoopes. Chapel Hill, NC: University of North Carolina Press, 1991.

Polan, Dana. *Scenes of Instruction: The Beginnings of the U.S. Study of Film*. Berkeley, CA: University of California Press, 2007.

Sarris, Andrew. *The American Cinema: Directors and Directions 1929–1968*. New York: Da Capo, 1996.

Shklovsky, Victor. *Theory of Prose*. Trans. Benjamin Sher. Elmwood Park, IL: Dalkey Archive Press, 1990.

Silver, Alain and James Ursini. *Film Noir Reader*. New York: Limelight Editions, 1996.

Taylor, Richard and Ian Christie, eds. *The Film Factory: Russian and Soviet Cinema in Documents, 1896–1939*. New York: Routledge, 1988.

Turvey, Malcolm. *The Filming of Modern Life: European Avant-Garde Film of the 1920s*. Cambridge, MA: MIT Press, 2011.

Vertov, Dziga. *Kino-Eye: The Writings of Dziga Vertov*. Trans. Kevin O'Brien. Ed. Annette Michelson. Berkeley, CA: University of California Press, 1984.

Wall-Romana, Christophe. *Jean Epstein*. New York: Manchester University Press, 2013.

Wasson, Haidee. *Museum Movies: The Museum of Modern Art and the Birth of Art Cinema*. Berkeley, CA: University of California Press, 2005.

Wiggershaus, Rolf. *The Frankfurt School: Its History, Theories, and Political Significance*. Trans. Michael Robertson. Cambridge, MA: MIT Press, 1994.

Winston, Brian. *Claiming the Real: The Documentary Film Revisited*. London: BFI, 2001.

CHAPTER 2: FRENCH THEORY, 1949–68

Althusser, Louis. *Lenin and Philosophy and Other Essays*. Trans. Ben Brewster. New York: Monthly Review, 2001.

Barthes, Roland. *Mythologies*. Trans. Annette Lavers. New York: Hill and Wang, 1972.

——. *Image/Music/Text*. Trans. Stephen Heath. New York: Hill and Wang, 1977.

Baudry, Jean-Louis. "Ideological Effects of the Basic Cinematographic Apparatus." Trans. Alan Williams. *Film Quarterly*, Vol. 28, No. 2 (Winter 1974–5): 39–47.

———. "The Apparatus: Metapsychological Approaches to the Impression of Reality in the Cinema." Trans. Jean Andrews and Bertrand Augst. *Camera Obscura*, Vol. 1, No. 1 (Fall 1976): 104–126.

Bellour, Raymond. *The Analysis of Film.* Ed. Constance Penley. Bloomington, IN: Indiana University Press, 2000.

Bergstrom, Janet, ed. *Endless Night: Cinema and Psychoanalysis, Parallel Histories.* Berkeley, CA: University of California Press, 1999.

Browne, Nick. *The Rhetoric of Filmic Narration.* Ann Arbor, MI: UMI Research Press, 1976.

Cahiers du cinéma editors. "John Ford's *Young Mr. Lincoln.*" Trans. Helen Lackner and Diana Matias. *Screen*, Vol. 13, No. 3 (Autumn 1972): 5–44.

Clarke, Simon. *The Foundations of Structuralism: A Critique of Lévi-Strauss and the Structuralist Movement.* Sussex: Harvester Press, 1981.

Comolli, Jean-Louis and Jean Narboni. "Cinema/Ideology/Criticism." Trans. Susan Bennett. *Screen*, Vol. 12, No. 1 (Spring 1971): 27–38.

Cusset, François. *French Theory: How Foucault, Derrida, Deleuze, & Co. Transformed the Intellectual Life of the United States.* Trans. Jeff Fort. Minneapolis, MN: University of Minnesota Press, 2008.

Dayan, Daniel. "The Tutor-Code of Classical Cinema." *Movies and Methods, Volume I.* Ed. Bill Nichols. Berkeley, CA: University of California Press, 1976. 438–451.

Debord, Guy. *The Society of the Spectacle.* Trans. Donald Nicholson-Smith. New York: Zone Books, 1995.

Donald, James, Anne Friedberg, and Luara Macus, eds. *Close Up 1927–1933: Cinema and Modernism.* Princeton, NJ: Princeton University Press, 1998.

Dosse, François. *History of Structuralism, Volume I: The Rising Sign, 1945–1966.* Trans. Deborah Glassman. Minneapolis, MN: University of Minnesota Press, 1997.

During, Simon, ed. *The Cultural Studies Reader.* 3rd ed. New York: Routledge, 2010.

Eco, Umberto. "Articulations of the Cinematic Code." *Movies and Methods, Volume I.* Ed. Bill Nichols. Berkeley, CA: University of California Press, 1976. 590–607.

Foucault, Michel. *Discipline and Punish: The Birth of the Prison.* Trans. Alan Sheridan. New York: Vintage Books, 1977.

Freud, Sigmund. *The Freud Reader.* Ed. Peter Gay. New York: W. W. Norton, 1989.

Gallop, Jane. *Reading Lacan.* Ithaca, NY: Cornell University Press, 1985.

Gitlin, Todd. *The Sixties: Years of Hope, Days of Rage*. New York: Bantam Books, 1987.

Graham, Peter and Ginette Vincendeau, eds. *The French New Wave: Critical Landmarks*. London: BFI, 2009.

Gramsci, Antonio. *Selections from the Prison Notebooks*. Eds. and trans. Quintin Hoare and Geoffrey Nowell Smith. New York: International Publishers, 2003.

Gutting, Gary. *French Philosophy in the Twentieth Century*. Cambridge: Cambridge University Press, 2001.

Hall, Stuart, Dorothy Hobson, Andrew Lowe, and Paul Willis, eds. *Culture, Media, Language: Working Papers in Cultural Studies, 1972–79*. New York: Routledge, 1996.

Harvey, Sylvia. *May '68 and Film Culture*. London: BFI, 1980.

Heath, Stephen. "Film and System: Terms of Analysis Part I." *Screen*, Vol. 16, No. 1 (Spring 1975): 7–77.

——. "Film and System: Terms of Analysis Part II." *Screen*, Vol. 16, No. 2 (Summer 1975): 91–113.

Home, Stewart, ed. *What Is Situationism? A Reader*. San Francisco, CA: AK Press, 1996.

James, David E. *Allegories of Cinema: American Film in the Sixties*. Princeton, NJ: Princeton University Press, 1989.

Jameson, Fredric. *The Prison-House of Language: A Critical Account of Structuralism and Russian Formalism*. Princeton, NJ: Princeton University Press, 1972.

Kauppi, Niilo. *French Intellectual Nobility: Institutional and Symbolic Transformations in the Post-Sartrian Era*. New York: State University of New York Press, 1996.

——. *Radicalism in French Culture: A Sociology of French Theory in the 1960s*. Burlington, VT: Ashgate, 2010.

Lacan, Jacques. *The Language of the Self: The Function of Language in Psychoanalysis*. Trans. Anthony Wilden. Baltimore, MD: Johns Hopkins University Press, 1968.

——. *Écrits: A Selection*. Trans. Bruce Fink. New York: Hill and Wang, 2002.

Lévi-Strauss, Claude. *Structural Anthropology*. Trans. Claire Jacobson and Brooke Grundfest Schoepf. New York: Basic Books, 1963.

——. *The Elementary Structures of Kinship*. Trans. James Harle Bell, John Richard von Sturmer, and Rodney Needham. Boston, MA: Beacon Press, 1969.

Lotringer, Sylvère and Sande Cohen, eds. *French Theory in America*. New York: Routledge, 2001.

MacCabe, Colin. *Godard: A Portrait of the Artist at Seventy*. New York: Faber and Faber, 2003.

Macey, David. *Lacan in Contexts*. New York: Verso, 1988.

Macksey, Richard and Eugenio Donato, eds. *The Structuralist Controversy: The Languages of Criticism and the Sciences of Man*. Baltimore, MD: Johns Hopkins University Press, 1972.

Marx, Karl. *Karl Marx: Selected Writings*. Ed. David McLellan. New York: Oxford University Press, 1977.

Metz, Christian. *Film Language: A Semiotics of the Cinema*. Trans. Michael Taylor. Chicago, IL: University of Chicago Press, 1974.

———. *Language and Cinema*. Trans. Donna Jean Umiker-Sebeok. The Hague: Mouton, 1974.

———. *The Imaginary Signifier: Psychoanalysis and the Cinema*. Trans. Celia Britton, Annwyl Williams, Ben Brewster, and Alfred Guzzetti. Bloomington, IN: Indiana University Press, 1982.

Miller, Jacques-Alain. "Suture (Elements of the Logic of the Signifier)." Trans. Jacqueline Rose. *Screen*, Vol. 18, No. 4 (Winter 1977): 24–34.

Oudart, Jean-Pierre. "Cinema and Suture." Trans. Kari Hanet. *Screen*, Vol. 18, No. 4 (Winter 1977): 35–47.

Pasolini, Pier Paolo. "The Cinema of Poetry." Trans. Marianne de Vettimo and Jacques Bontemps. *Movies and Methods, Volume I*. Ed. Bill Nichols. Berkeley, CA: University of California, 1976. 542–558.

Rodowick, D. N. *The Crisis of Political Modernism: Criticism and Ideology in Contemporary Film Theory*. Berkeley, CA: University of California, 1994.

Roudinesco, Elisabeth. *Jacques Lacan*. Trans. Barbara Bray. New York: Columbia University Press, 1997.

Sanders, Carol. *The Cambridge Companion to Saussure*. Cambridge: Cambridge University Press, 2004.

Saussure, Ferdinand de. *Course in General Linguistics*. Trans. Wade Baskin. Eds. Charles Bally and Albert Sechehaye. New York: McGraw-Hill, 1959.

Silverman, Kaja. *The Subject of Semiotics*. New York: Oxford University Press, 1983.

Spottiswoode, Raymond. *A Grammar of the Film: An Analysis of Film Technique*. Berkeley, CA: University of California Press, 1950.

Thompson, Duncan. *Pessimism of the Intellect? A History of New Left Review*. Monmouth: Merlin Press, 2007.

Turner, Graeme. *British Cultural Studies: An Introduction*. Boston, MA: Unwin Hyman, 1990.

Weber, Samuel. *Return to Freud: Jacques Lacan's Dislocation of Psychoanalysis*. Trans. Michael Levine. Cambridge: Cambridge University Press, 1992.

Williams, Linda. *Figures of Desire: A Theory and Analysis of Surrealist Film*. Berkeley, CA: University of California Press, 1981.

CHAPTER 3: SCREEN THEORY, 1969–96

Adams, Parveen and Elizabeth Cowie, eds. *The Woman in Question*: m/f. Cambridge, MA: MIT Press, 1990.

Altman, Rick. *Film/Genre*. London: BFI, 1999.

Bad Object-Choices, ed. *How Do I Look? Queer Film and Video*. Seattle, WA: Bay Press, 1991.

Barthes, Roland. *S/Z: An Essay*. Trans. Richard Miller. New York: Hill and Wang, 1974.

Baudrillard, Jean. *Simulacra and Simulation*. Trans. Sheila Faria Glaser. Ann Arbor, MI: University of Michigan Press, 1994.

Benshofff, Harry M. and Sean Griffin. *Queer Images: A History of Gay and Lesbian Film in America*. New York: Rowman and Littlefield, 2006.

Bhabha, Homi K. *The Location of Culture*. New York: Routledge, 1994.

Bolas, Terry. *Screen Education: From Film Appreciation to Media Studies*. Chicago, IL: Intellect, 2009.

Bordwell, David, Janet Staiger, and Kristin Thompson. *The Classical Hollywood Cinema: Film Style and Mode of Production to 1960*. New York: Columbia University Press, 1985.

Buckland, Warren. *Film Theory: Rational Reconstructions*. New York: Routledge, 2012.

Butler, Judith. *Gender Trouble: Feminism and the Subversion of Identity*. New York: Routledge, 1999.

Chion, Michel. *The Voice and Cinema*. Trans. Claudia Gorbman. New York: Columbia University Press, 1999.

Clover, Carol J. *Men, Women, and Chain Saws: Gender in the Modern Horror Film*. Princeton, NJ: Princeton University Press, 1992.

Cowie, Elizabeth. *Representing the Woman: Cinema and Psychoanalysis*. Minneapolis, MN: University of Minnesota Press, 1997.

de Beauvoir, Simone. *The Second Sex*. Trans. Constance Borde and Sheila Malovany-Chevallier. New York: Vintage, 2011.

de Lauretis, Teresa. *Alice Doesn't: Feminism, Semiotics, Cinema*. Bloomington, IN: Indiana University Press, 1984.

——. *The Practice of Love: Lesbian Sexuality and Perverse Desire*. Bloomington, IN: Indiana University Press, 1994.

de Lauretis, Teresa and Stephen Heath, eds. *The Cinematic Apparatus*. New York: St. Martin's Press, 1980.

Derrida, Jacques. "Différance." *Margins of Philosophy*. Trans. Alan Bass. Chicago, IL: University of Chicago Press, 1982.

Dicker, Rory. *A History of U.S. Feminisms*. Berkeley, CA: Seal Press, 2008.

Doane, Mary Ann. *The Desire to Desire: The Woman's Film of the 1940s*. Bloomington, IN: Indiana University Press, 1987.

Dyer, Richard. "Entertainment and Utopia." *Movies and Methods, Volume II*. Ed. Bill Nichols. Berkeley, CA: University of California, 1985. 220–232.

Fanon, Frantz. *The Wretched of the Earth*. Trans. Richard Philcox. New York: Grove Press, 1961.

——. *Black Skin, White Masks*. Trans. Charles Lam Markmann. New York: Grove Press, 1967.

Foster, Hal, ed. *The Anti-Aesthetic: Essays on Postmodern Culture*. New York: New Press, 1998.

Foucault, Michel. *The History of Sexuality: An Introduction, Volume I*. Trans. Robert Hurely. New York: Vintage Books, 1978.

Friedan, Betty. *The Feminine Mystique*. New York: W. W. Norton, 1963.

Gever, Martha, John Greyson, and Pratibha Parmar, eds. *Queer Looks: Perspectives on Lesbian and Gay Film and Video*. New York: Routledge, 1993.

Gidal, Peter, ed. *Structural Film Anthology*. London: BFI, 1978.

Grievson, Lee and Haidee Wasson, eds. *Inventing Film Studies*. Durham: Duke University Press, 2008.

Hansen, Miriam. *Babel and Babylon: Spectatorship in American Silent Film*. Cambridge, MA: Harvard University Press, 1991.

Haraway, Donna. *Simians, Cyborgs, and Women: The Reinvention of Nature*. New York: Routledge, 1991.

Haskell, Molly. *From Reverence to Rape: The Treatment of Women in the Movies*. 2nd ed. Chicago, IL: University of Chicago Press, 1987.

Heath, Stephen. *Questions of Cinema*. Bloomington, IN: Indiana University Press, 1981.

Heath, Stephen and Patricia Mellencamp. *Cinema and Language*. Los Angeles, CA: American Film Institute, 1983.

Hollinger, Karen. *Feminist Film Studies*. New York: Routledge, 2012.

hooks, bell. *Black Looks: Race and Representation*. Boston, MA: South End Press, 1992.

Jameson, Fredric. *The Political Unconscious: Narrative as a Socially Symbolic Act*. Ithaca, NY: Cornell University Press, 1981.

——. *Postmodernism or, The Cultural Logic of Late Capitalism*. Durham: Duke University Press, 1991.

Kaplan, E. Ann, ed. *Feminism and Film*. New York: Oxford University Press, 2000.

Kristeva, Julia. *Powers of Horror: An Essay on Abjection*. Trans. Leon S. Roudiez. New York: Columbia University Press, 1982.

Lesage, Julia. "The Human Subject: He, She, or Me? (or, the Case of the Missing Penis)." *Jump Cut*, No. 4 (1974): 26–27. www.ejumpcut.org/archive/onlinessays/JC04folder/ScreenReviewed.

Lorde, Audre. *Sister Outsider: Essays and Speeches*. Freedom, CA: Crossing Press, 1984.

Lyotard, Jean-François. *The Postmodern Condition: A Report on Knowledge*. Trans. Geoff Bennington and Brian Massumi. Minneapolis, MN: University of Minnesota Press, 1984.

MacBean, James. *Film and Revolution*. Bloomington, IN: Indiana University Press, 1975.

MacCabe, Colin. "Realism and the Cinema: Notes on some Brechtian Theses." *Screen*, Vol. 15, No. 2 (Summer 1974): 7–27.

——. "Theory and Film: Principles of Realism and Pleasure." *Screen*, Vol. 17, No. 3 (Autumn 1976): 7–28.

——. *Tracking the Signifier: Theoretical Essays: Film, Linguistics, Literature.* Minneapolis, MN: University of Minnesota Press, 1985.

Marks, Laura U. *The Skin of the Film: Intercultural Cinema, Embodiment, and the Senses.* Durham, NC: Duke University Press, 2000.

Mayne, Judith. *The Woman at the Keyhole: Feminism and Women's Cinema.* Bloomington, IN: Indiana University Press, 1990.

——. *Cinema and Spectatorship.* New York: Routledge, 1993.

Menand, Louis. *The Marketplace of Ideas: Reform and Resistance in the American University.* New York: W. W. Norton, 2010.

Millet, Kate. *Sexual Politics.* New York: Ballantine, 1970.

Mitchell, Juliet. *Psychoanalysis and Feminism: A Radical Reassessment of Freudian Psychoanalysis.* New York: Basic Books, 1974.

Mitry, Jean. *The Aesthetics and Psychology of the Cinema.* Trans. Christopher King. Bloomington, IN: Indiana University Press, 1997.

Modleski, Tania. *Loving with a Vengeance: Mass-Produced Fantasies for Women.* New York: Routledge, 1990.

——. *The Women Who Knew Too Much: Hitchcock and Feminist Theory.* New York: Routledge, 1988.

Naficy, Hamid. *An Accented Cinema: Exilic and Diasporic Filmmaking.* Princeton, NJ: Princeton University Press, 2001.

Nichols, Bill. *Representing Reality: Issues and Concepts in Documentary.* Bloomington, IN: Indiana University Press, 1991.

——. *Blurred Boundaries: Questions of Meaning in Contemporary Culture.* Bloomington, IN: Indiana University Press, 1994.

Oliver, Kelly, ed. *French Feminism Reader.* New York: Rowman and Littlefield, 2000.

Penley, Constance, ed. *Feminism and Film Theory.* New York: Routledge, 1988.

Pines, Jim and Paul Willemen, eds. *Questions of Third Cinema.* London: BFI, 1989.

Readings, Bill. *The University in Ruins.* Cambridge, MA: Harvard University Press, 1996.

Rodowick, D. N. *The Difficulty of Difference: Psychoanalysis, Sexual Difference, and Film Theory.* New York: Routledge, 1991.

Rogin, Michael. *Blackface, White Noise: Jewish Immigrants in the Hollywood Melting Pot.* Berkeley, CA: University of California Press, 1996.

Rosen, Marjorie. *Popcorn Venus: Women, Movies, and the American Dream.* New York: Coward, McCann, and Geoghegan, 1973.

Said, Edward W. *Orientalism.* New York: Vintage Books, 1978.

Sartre, Jean-Paul. *Anti-Semite and Jew.* Trans. George J. Becker. New York: Schocken Books, 1948.

Shohat, Ella and Robert Stam. *Unthinking Eurocentrism: Multiculturalism and the Media*. New York: Routledge, 1994.

Silverman, Kaja. *The Acoustic Mirror: The Female Voice in Psychoanalysis and Cinema*. Bloomington, IN: Indiana University Press, 1988.

——. *Male Subjectivity at the Margins*. New York: Routledge, 1992.

Solanas, Fernando and Octavio Getino. "Towards a Third Cinema." *Movies and Methods, Volume 1*. Ed. Bill Nichols. Berkeley, CA: University of Berkeley, 1976. 44–64.

Spivak, Gayatri Chakravorty. "Can the Subaltern Speak?" *Marxism and the Interpretation of Culture*. Eds. Cary Nelson and Lawrence Grossberg. Urbana, IL: University of Illinois Press, 1988. 271–313.

Stam, Robert, Robert Burgoyne, and Sandy Flitterman-Lewis. *New Vocabularies in Film Semiotics: Structuralism, Post-Structuralism, and Beyond*. New York: Routledge, 1992.

Sullivan, Nikki. *A Critical Introduction to Queer Theory*. New York: New York University Press, 2003.

Thornham, Sue. *Feminist Film Theory: A Reader*. New York: New York University Press, 1999.

Trinh T., Minh-ha. *Woman, Native, Other: Writing, Postcoloniality, and Feminism*. Bloomington, IN: Indiana University Press, 1989.

——. *Framer Framed*. New York: Routledge, 1992.

Turim, Maureen. "Gentlemen Consume Blondes." *Movies and Methods, Volume 2*. Ed. Bill Nichols. Berkeley, CA: University of California, 1985. 369–378.

Williams, Linda. *Hard Core: Power, Pleasure, and the "Frenzy of the Visible."* Berkeley, CA: University of California Press, 1989.

Wollen, Peter. *Signs and Meaning in the Cinema*. Bloomington, IN: Indiana University Press, 1972.

——. *Readings and Writings: Semiotic Counter-Strategies*. London: Verso, 1982.

CHAPTER 4: POST-THEORY, 1996–2015

"About October." *October* 1 (Spring 1976): 3–5.

Agamben, Giorgio. *Homo Sacer: Sovereign Power and Bare Life*. Trans. Daniel Heller-Roazen. Stanford, CA: Stanford University Press, 1998.

Allen, Richard. *Projecting Illusion: Film Spectatorship and the Impression of Reality*. Cambridge: Cambridge University Press, 1995.

Allen, Richard and Murray Smith, eds. *Film Theory and Philosophy*. New York: Oxford University Press, 1999.

Andrew, Dudley. *What Cinema Is! Bazin's Quest and Its Charge*. Malden, MA: Blackwell, 2010.

Badiou, Alain. *Cinema*. Ed. Antoine de Baecque. Trans. Susan Spitzer. Malden, MA: Polity, 2013.

Balio, Tino. *Hollywood in the New Millennium*. London: BFI, 2013.

Beller, Jonathan. *The Cinematic Mode of Production: Attention Economy and the Society of the Spectacle*. Hanover, NH: Dartmouth College Press, 2006.

Bolter, Jay David and Richard Grusin. *Remediation: Understanding New Media*. Cambridge, MA: MIT Press, 2000.

Bordwell, David. *Narration in the Fiction Film*. Madison, WI: University of Wisconsin Press, 1985.

——. *Ozu and the Poetics of Cinema*. Princeton, NJ: Princeton University Press, 1988.

——. "Adventures in the Highlands of Theory." *Screen*, Vol. 29, No. 1 (Winter 1988): 72–97.

——. *Making Meaning: Inference and Rhetoric in the Interpretation of Cinema*. Cambridge, MA: Harvard University Press, 1989.

——. "A Case for Cognitivism." *Iris* No. 9 (Spring 1989): 11–40.

——. "Historical Poetics of Cinema." *The Cinematic Text: Methods and Approaches*. Ed. R. Barton Palmer. New York: AMS Press, 1989.

——. "Preaching Pluralism: Pluralism, Truth, and Scholarly Inquiry in Film Studies." *Cinema Journal*, Vol. 37, No. 2 (Winter 1998): 84–90.

——. *Planet Hong Kong: Popular Cinema and the Art of Entertainment*. Cambridge, MA: Harvard University Press, 2003.

——. *The Way Hollywood Tells It: Story and Style in Modern Movies*. Berkeley, CA: University of California, 2006.

——. *Poetics of Cinema*. New York: Routledge, 2008.

Bordwell, David and Noël Carroll, eds. *Post-Theory: Reconstructing Film Studies*. Madison, WI: University of Wisconsin Press, 1996.

Branigan, Edward. *Narrative Comprehension and Film*. New York: Routledge, 1992.

Brown, William. *Supercinema: Film-Philosophy for the Digital Age*. New York: Berghahn, 2013.

Brunette, Peter and David Wills. *Screen/Play: Derrida and Film Theory*. Princeton, NJ: Princeton University Press, 1989.

Buckland, Warren. "Critique of Poor Reason." *Screen*, Vol. 30, No. 4 (Autumn 1989): 80–103.

——. *The Cognitive Semiotics of Film*. Cambridge: Cambridge University Press, 2004.

Carroll, Noël. "Address to the Heathen." *October* 23 (Winter 1982): 89–163.

——. "A Reply to Heath." *October* 27 (Winter 1983): 81–102.

——. *Mystifying Movies: Fads and Fallacies in Contemporary Film Theory*. New York: Columbia University Press, 1988.

————. *Philosophical Problems of Classical Film Theory*. Princeton, NJ: Princeton University Press, 1988b.

————. "Cognitivism, Contemporary Film Theory and Method: A Response to Warren Buckland." *Journal of Dramatic Theory and Criticism*, Vol. 6, No. 2 (Spring 1992): 199–220.

Cavell, Stanley. *The World Viewed: Reflections on the Ontology of Film*. Cambridge, MA: Harvard University Press, 1971.

Colman, Felicity, ed. *Film, Theory, and Philosophy: The Key Thinkers*. Montreal: McGill-Queen's University Press, 2009.

Crary, Jonathan. *Techniques of the Observer: On Vision and Modernity in the 19th Century*. Cambridge, MA: MIT Press, 1992.

Cubitt, Sean. *The Cinema Effect*. Cambridge, MA: MIT Press, 2004.

Deleuze, Gilles. *Cinema 1: The Movement-Image*. Trans. Hugh Tomlinson and Barbara Habberjam. Minneapolis, MN: University of Minnesota Press, 1986.

————. *Cinema 2: The Time-Image*. Trans. Hugh Tomlinson and Robert Galeta. Minneapolis, MN: University of Minnesota Press, 1989.

Elsaesser, Thomas, ed. *Early Cinema: Space, Frame, Narrative*. London: BFI, 1990.

Flaxman, Gregory, ed. *The Brain Is the Screen: Deleuze and the Philosophy of Cinema*. Minneapolis, MN: University of Minnesota Press, 2000.

Galloway, Alexander. *The Interface Effect*. Malden, MA: Polity, 2012.

Gitelman, Lisa. *Always Already New: Media, History, and the Data of Culture*. Cambridge, MA: MIT Press, 2008.

Harries, Dan. *The New Media Book*. London: BFI, 2002.

Heath, Stephen. "Le Père Noël." *October* 26 (Autumn 1983): 63–115.

Henderson, Brian. *A Critique of Film Theory*. New York: E. P. Dutton, 1980.

Jenkins, Henry. *Convergence Culture: Where Old and New Media Collide*. New York: New York University, 2006.

Jeong, Seung-Hoon. *Cinematic Interfaces: Film Theory after New Media*. New York: Routledge, 2013.

King, Barry. "The Story Continues . . . " *Screen*, Vol. 28, No. 3 (Summer 1987): 56–83.

Kittler, Friedrich. *Gramophone, Film, Typewriter*. Trans. Geoffrey Winthrop-Young and Michael Wutz. Stanford, CA: Stanford University Press, 1999.

Lehman, Peter. "Pluralism Versus the Correct Position." *Cinema Journal*, Vol. 36, No. 2 (Winter 1997): 114–119.

Lippit, Akira Mizuta. *Atomic Light (Shadow Optics)*. Minneapolis, MN: University of Minnesota Press, 2005.

Manovich, Lev. *The Language of New Media*. Cambridge, MA: MIT Press, 2001.

McDonald, Paul and Janet Wasko, eds. *The Contemporary Hollywood Film Industry*. Malden, MA: Blackwell, 2008.

McGowan, Todd. *The Real Gaze: Film Theory After Lacan*. New York: State University of New York, 2007.

——. *Out of Time: Desire in Atemporal Cinema*. Minneapolis, MN: University of Minnesota Press, 2011.

McGowan, Todd and Sheila Kunkle, eds. *Lacan and Contemporary Film*. New York: Other Press, 2004.

Muller, John P. and William J. Richardson, eds. *The Purloined Poe: Lacan, Derrida, and Psychoanalytic Reading*. Baltimore, MD: Johns Hopkins University Press, 1988.

Perkins, V. F. *Film as Film: Understanding and Judging Movies*. New York: Penguin Books, 1972.

Pisters, Patricia. *The Neuro-Image: A Deleuzian Film-Philosophy of Digital Screen Culture*. Stanford, CA: Stanford University Press, 2012.

Plantinga, Carl. "Cognitive Film Theory: An Insider's Appraisal." *Cinémas: Revue d'Études Cinématographiques*, Vol. 12, No. 2 (Winter 2002): 15–37.

——. *Moving Viewers: American Film and the Spectator's Experience*. Berkeley, CA: University of California Press, 2009.

Rancière, Jacques. *Film Fables*. Trans. Emiliano Battista. New York: Berg, 2006.

——. *The Future of the Image*. Trans. Gregory Elliot. New York: Verso, 2007.

——. *The Emancipated Spectator*. Trans. Gregory Elliot. New York: Verso, 2007.

Rich, Ruby B., Chuck Kleinhans, and Julia Lesage. "Report on a Conference Not Attended: The Scalpel Beneath the Suture." *Jump Cut*, No. 17 (April 1978): 37–38. www.ejumpcut.org/archive/onlinessays/JC17 folder/ConfNotAttended.

Rodowick, D. N. *Gilles Deleuze's Time Machine*. Durham, NC: Duke University Press, 1997.

——. *Reading the Figural, or, Philosophy after the New Media*. Durham, NC: Duke University Press, 2001.

——. *The Virtual Life of Film*. Cambridge, MA: Harvard University Press, 2007.

——. "An Elegy for Theory." *October* 122 (Fall 2007): 91–109.

——. *Elegy for Theory*. Cambridge, MA: Harvard University Press, 2014.

Rodowick, D. N., ed. *Afterimages of Gilles Deleuze's Film Philosophy*. Minneapolis, MN: University of Minnesota Press, 2010.

Silverman, Kaja. *The Threshold of the Visible World*. New York: Routledge, 1996.

Sobchack, Vivian. *The Address of the Eye: A Phenomenology of Film Experience*. Princeton, NJ: Princeton University Press, 1992.

Stewart, Garrett. *Framed Time: Toward a Postfilmic Cinema*. Chicago, IL: University of Chicago Press, 2007.

Thompson, Kristin. *Breaking the Glass Armor: Neoformalist Film Analysis*. Princeton, NJ: Princeton University Press, 1988.

Virilio, Paul. *War and Cinema: The Logistics of Perception*. Trans. Patrick Camiller. New York: Verso, 1989.

Žižek, Slavoj. *The Sublime Object of Ideology*. New York: Verso, 1989.

——. *Looking Awry: An Introduction to Jacques Lacan through Popular Culture*. Cambridge, MA: MIT Press, 1991.

——. *Enjoy Your Symptom! Jacques Lacan in Hollywood and Out*. New York: Routledge, 1992.

——. *The Fright of Real Tears: Krzysztof Kieslowski Between Theory and Post-Theory*. London: BFI, 2001.

Žižek, Slavoj, ed. *Everything You Always Wanted to Know About Lacan . . . But Were Afraid to Ask Hitchcock*. New York: Verso, 1992.

GENERAL SOURCES: INTRODUCTORY TEXTS

Andrew, Dudley. *The Major Film Theories: An Introduction*. New York: Oxford University Press, 1976.

——. *Concepts in Film Theory*. New York: Oxford University Press, 1984.

Casetti, Francesco. *Theories of Cinema, 1945–1995*. Trans. Francesca Chiostri and Elizabeth Gard Bartolini-Salimbeni with Thomas Kelso. Austin, TX: University of Texas, 1999.

Elsaesser, Thomas and Malte Hagener. *Film Theory: An Introduction through the Senses*. New York: Routledge, 2010.

Lapsley, Robert and Michael Westlake. *Film Theory: An Introduction*. 2nd ed. New York: Manchester University Press, 2006.

Moncao, James. *How to Read a Film: The Art, Technology, Language, History and Theory of Film and Media*. Revised edition. New York: Oxford University Press, 1981.

Rushton, Richard and Gary Bettinson. *What is Film Theory? An Introduction to Contemporary Debates*. New York: Open University Press, 2010.

Stam, Robert. *Film Theory: An Introduction*. Malden, MA: Blackwell, 2000.

Tredell, Nicolas, ed. *Cinemas of the Mind: A Critical History of Film Theory*. Cambridge: Totem Books, 2002.

GENERAL SOURCES: ANTHOLOGIES AND COLLECTIONS

Branigan, Edward and Warren Buckland, eds. *The Routledge Encyclopedia of Film Theory*. New York: Routledge, 2014.

Braudy, Leo, ed. *Film Theory and Criticism: Introductory Readings*. 7th ed. New York: Oxford University Press, 2009.

Cook, Pam, ed. *The Cinema Book*. 3rd ed. London: BFI, 2007.

Hill, John and Pamela Church Gibson, eds. *The Oxford Guide to Film Studies*. New York: Oxford University Press, 1998.

Miller, Toby and Robert Stam, eds. *A Companion to Film Theory*. Malden, MA: Blackwell, 2004.

Nichols, Bill, ed. *Movies and Methods Volume I*. Berkeley, CA: University of California Press, 1976.

——. *Movies and Methods Volume II*. Berkeley, CA: University of California Press, 1985.

Rosen, Philip, ed. *Narrative, Apparatus, Ideology: A Film Theory Reader*. New York: Columbia University Press, 1986.

Stam, Robert and Toby Miller, eds. *Film and Theory: An Anthology*. Malden, MA: Blackwell, 2000.

INDEX